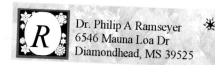
THE MEDIEVAL AND EARLY MODERN WORLD

PRIMARY SOURCES AND REFERENCE VOLUME

BONNIE G. SMITH
GENERAL EDITOR

THE MEDIEVAL AND EARLY MODERN WORLD

PRIMARY SOURCES AND REFERENCE VOLUME

Donald R. Kelley and Bonnie G. Smith

OXFORD
UNIVERSITY PRESS

To P., P., and J.

OXFORD
UNIVERSITY PRESS

Oxford University Press, Inc., publishes works that further
Oxford University's objective of excellence
in research, scholarship, and education.

Oxford New York
Auckland Cape Town Dar es Salaam Hong Kong Karachi
Kuala Lumpur Madrid Melbourne Mexico City Nairobi
New Delhi Shanghai Taipei Toronto

With offices in
Argentina Austria Brazil Chile Czech Republic France Greece
Guatemala Hungary Italy Japan Poland Portugal Singapore
South Korea Switzerland Thailand Turkey Ukraine Vietnam

Published by Oxford University Press, Inc.
198 Madison Avenue, New York, New York 10016
www.oup.com

Series design: Stephanie Blumenthal
Volume layout: Mary Neal Meador
Cover design and logo: Nora Wertz

Library of Congress Cataloging-in-Publication Data

The medieval & early modern world : primary sources and reference
volume / [edited by] Donald R. Kelley and Bonnie G. Smith.
p. cm. -- (The medieval & early modern world)
Consists chiefly of primary source material and also includes an index to the other six titles in the series.
Includes bibliographical references and indexes.

1. Middle Ages--History--Sources. 2. History, Modern--16th century--Sources. 3. History, Modern--17th century--
Sources. 4. Medieval and early modern world--Indexes. 5. Middle Ages--History--Juvenile literature--Indexes.
6. History, Modern--16th century--Juvenile literature--Indexes. 7. History, Modern--17th century--Juvenile literature--
Indexes. I. Title: Medieval and early modern world. II. Smith, Bonnie G., 1940- III. Kelley, Donald R.,
1931- IV. Medieval and early modern world.
D101.2.M34 2005
909.07--dc22
2004029387
ISBN-13: 978-0-19-522157-2 (set)
ISBN-10: 0-19-522157-5 (set)

Printing number: 9 8 7 6 5 4 3 2 1

Printed in the United States of America
on acid-free paper

On the cover: This porcelain figure of a well-dressed young man writing a letter
to his ladylove was made in Germany about 1745.
Frontispiece: The mapmaker Giovanni Leardo oriented this 1442 world map with east at the top.

BONNIE G. SMITH
GENERAL EDITOR

DIANE L. BROOKS, ED.D.
EDUCATION CONSULTANT

CONTENTS

A 🙶 *marks a primary source—a piece of writing that speaks to us from the past.*

CAST OF CHARACTERS

'Abd ul-Qadir (abd-UHL-kah-DEER) Bada'uni (bah-dah-OO-nee), 1540–about 1615 • Islamic historian who wrote a *History of Mughal India*

Abu 'Abd Allah (uh-BOO abd AH-luh) Muhammad (moo-HAH-mud) al-sharif (al-shah-REEF) al-Idrisi (al-ih-DREE-see), 11th century • North African traveler who wrote accurate books of geography

Abu'l-Tayyib (uh-BOOL-tie-YEEB) Ahmad (ah-MAHD) ibn al-Husayn (ih-bin al-hoo-SAYN) al-Dju'fi (al-JOO-fee) al-Mutanabbi (al-moo-TAHN-ah-bee), 915–965 • official court poet of the Middle Eastern ruler Saif al-Dawla

Abu 'Ubayd (uh-BOO oo-BIED) 'Abd Allah (abd AH-luh) bin 'Abd al-'Aziz (bin abd al-ah-ZEEZ) al-Bakri (al-BACK-ree), 11th century • Spanish author who wrote some of the best geography books of his day

Akbar (AHK-bahr), 1542–1605 • 16th-century ruler of the Mughal Empire in India

'Ala-ad-Din (a-lah-ad-din) 'Ata-Malik (ah-tah-mah-LEEK) Juvaini (joo-VINE-nee), 1226–1283 • Muslim author who wrote a history of the Mongols

al-Bakri. *See* Abu 'Ubayd 'Abd Allah bin 'Abd al-'Aziz al-Bakri

al-Idrisi. *See* Abu 'Abd Allah Muhammad al-sharif al-Idrisi

al-Mas'udi (al-mahs-OO-dee), 10th century • Arabic traveler and historian who kept a journal of his travels around the Indian Ocean

Askia (as-KEE-yuh) Muhammad (moo-HAH-mud), ruled 1493–1528 • ruler of the Songhay Empire in Mali

Arthur, King • legendary ruler of Britain; subject of many myths and stories

Benjamin of Tudela (too-DAY-lah), about 1127–1173 • Spanish rabbi who wrote about his travels to the Middle East

Calvin, John, 1509–1564 • French Protestant leader

Cervantes (sehr-VAHN-tays), Miguel de (mee-GEHL day), 1547–1616 • Spanish novelist; author of *Don Quixote*

Columbus, Christopher, 1451–1506 • Italian navigator and explorer for Spain

Confucius (con-FYU-shus), 551–about 479 BCE • Chinese philosopher and sage known to the Chinese as Kongzi, whose ideas have been important across East Asia and around the world down to the present

Cortés (cor-TESS), Hernán (err-NAHN), 1485–1547 • Spanish explorer who conquered the Aztec Empire

Cruz (crooz), Sor (sohr) (Sister) Juana Inés de la (HWAH-nah ee-NES day lah), 1648–1695 • a Mexican nun and poet known for her studiousness and writing

Dürer (DYUHR-uhr), Albrecht (AHL-brecht), 1471–1528 • a renowned German painter

Du (doo) Fu (foo), 712–790 • Chinese poet

Edward II, 1284–1327 • English king who summoned the Model Parliament

Erasmus (ih-RAZ-mus), Desiderius (deh-zih-DEHR-ee-us), about 1466–1536 • Dutch author, humanist, and religious reformer

Galland (ga-LAHN), Antoine (an-TWON), 1646–1715 • French author and translator

Gao (gaow) **Qi** (chee), 1336–1374
• Chinese poet

Gelasius I (jihl-EY-shee-us), active
492–496 • Pope who strongly
defended the power of the papacy
in Rome

Guenivere (GWEN-eh-veer) •
legendary wife of King Arthur

Hideyoshi (hih-day-OH-shee),
1536–1598 • a ruler of Japan with
great ambition for his country

Huili (hway-lee), seventh century
• the Buddhist pilgrim Xuanzang's
disciple and assistant, who wrote
the story of the monk's life

Isabella, 1451–1504 • queen of
Spain who sponsored exploration
of the New World and the
Inquisition to rid Spain of non-
Catholics

St. Jerome, 347–about 420 • a
founding father of the Catholic
Church.

John of Salisbury, about
1110–1180 • English bishop and
scholar who wrote about politics

Kant (KAHNT), **Immanuel** (ih-
MAN-oo-ehl), 1724–1804 •
German Enlightenment philoso-
pher

Louis XIV, 1643–1715 • king of
France, known as the Sun King

Luther, Martin, 1483–1546 •
German monk who is credited
with starting the Protestant
Reformation

Machiavelli (ma-kee-uh-VEH-lee),
Niccolò (NEE-ko-lo), 1469–1527
• Italian political writer; author of
The Prince

Magalotti (ma-ga-LO-tee), **Count
Lorenzo** (lohr-EHN-zo),
1637–1712 • Italian nobleman,
poet, and amateur scientist who
wrote about his travels with
Cosmo, the Grand Duke of
Tuscany

Mahmud (mah-MOOD) **Kati**
(KAH-tee), 16th century •
Renowned scholar from
Timbuktu, Mali, who wrote a his-
tory of Askia Muhammad's rule

Malory, Sir Thomas, 15th century
• British author of *Le Morte
d'Arthur* (The Death of Arthur)

Muhammad (moo-HAH-mud) **ibn
Asad Jalal** (ih-bin ah-SAHD jah-
LAHL) **ud-din al-Dawwani** (ood-
in al-duh-WAH-nee), 1426–1502 •
Persian moral philosopher

Muhammad (moo-HAH-mud)
Mujir (moo-JEER) **Wajib** (wah-
JEEB) **Adib** (AH-deeb), 14th century • Muslim author who wrote
a guide for converts to Islam

Munjong (MOON-johng),
1414–1452 • Korean king and
agricultural planner

Murasaki (muhr-uh-SAH-kee)
Shikibu (SHEE-kee-boo), about
978–about 1031 • author of the
Tale of Genji and inventor of the
novel in Japan

Omar (OH-mahr) **Khayyam** (kai-
YAHM), about 1048–1122 •
Persian poet and astronomer;
author of *Rubaiyat*

Pegolotti (peh-go-LO-tee),
Francesco di Balducci (fran-
CHES-ko dee bal-DOO-chee) •
banker from Florence who wrote
an advice book for merchants

Pepys (PEEPS), **Samuel**,
1633–1703 • English government
worker and diarist

Radishchev (ra-DEESH-chehv),
Alexander, 1749–1802 • Russian
Enlightenment nobleman and
author

Raymond of Agiles (ah-JEEL),
11th–12th centuries • French
clergyman, historian, and knight
who wrote an eyewitness account
of the capture Jerusalem in 1099
during the First Crusade

Ratanbai (rah-TAHN-bai), about
12th–14th centuries • South
Asian "bhakti" poet

Sejong (SEH-johng), 1397–1450 •
Korean king, father of Munjong

Snorrason (snohr-AH-son), **Oddr**
(AWDR), about 12th century •
Icelandic Benedictine monk and
author of Viking saga

Sorbon (sohr-BOHN), **Robert of**,
1201–1274 • royal councilor,
founder of French college that
became the oldest part of the
University of Paris

Sugita (soo-GEE-tah) Gempaku (gehm-PAH-ko), 18th century • Japanese doctor

Sultan Mehmed (MEH-meht) II, 1432–1481 • Ottoman Turkish conqueror who defeated the Byzantine Empire at Constantinople in 1453

Sundiata (suhn-dee-AH-tah) Keita (KAY-tah), d. about 1255 • legendary founder of the kingdom of Mali in West Africa

Toussaint L'Ouverture (TOO-sahn LOO-vehr-TUHR), Pierre Dominique (pee-AIR doh-meh-NEEK), about 1744–1803 • leader of slave revolt on Santo Domingo (modern-day Haiti)

Urban II, about 1035–1099 • pope who called for the First Crusade

Usama (yu-SAH-mah) ibn Munqidh (ih-bin muhn-KEED), 1095–1188 • Muslim author of "Memoirs," a record of his family and the arrival of the Christian Crusaders in the Holy Land

Xuanzang (shoo-EHN-zahng), b. 602 • Buddhist monk, renowned for his 10,000-mile pilgrimage through Asia in search of Buddhist texts; the basis for the character in *Journey to the West,* or *Monkey*

Wheatley, Phillis, about 1753–1784 • African-American poet who came to America from Senegal as a slave

Wu Cheng'en (woo chehng-EHN), about 1500–1582 • author of the Chinese epic loosely based on the life of Xuanzang *Journey to the West,* also known as *Monkey*

Zheng (jehng), Miss, eighth century • Confucian author of advice book for women

SOME PRONUNCIATIONS

Algiers (al-JEERS)

Avignon (ah-vee-NYON)

Azores (A-zohrs)

Beijing (bay-jing)

Borneo (BOR-nee-o)

Chang'an (chahng-ahn)

Damascus (duh-MASS-cus)

Ghana (GAH-nuh)

Hangyang (hahng-yahng)

Hangzhou (hahng-jo)

Heian-kyo (HAY-ahn-KEE-o)

Kabul (KAH-buhl)

Kilwa (KIL-way)

Mombasa (mahm-BAH-suh)

Mwenemutapa (Mweh-neh-moo-
TAH-pah)

Nanjing (nahn-jing)

Oyo (o-YO)

Punjab (puhn-JAHB)

Samarkand (SA-muhr-kand)

Songhay (sohn-GAI)

Sumatra (soo-MAH-truh)

Tenochtitlan (tay-NOTCH-tee-
TLAN)

Timbuktu (tihm-buhk-TOO)

Tunis (TOO-nuhs)

Vijayanagara (vih-juh-yuh-NUH-
guhr-uh)

Yangzi River (yahng-dzuh)

D

St.Petersburg

EUROPE
RUSSIA
ASIA

LAND
n
Antwerp
Kiev
Paris
Vienna
FRANCE
AUSTRIA
MONGOL EMPIRE
Avignon
Venice
Beijing
Florence
Samarkand
Hangyang
Rome
Constantinople
(Seoul)
JAPAN
Black Sea
Kabul
IN
OTTOMAN
SAFAVID
Huang He
Chang'an
KOREA
Sicily
EMPIRE
EMPIRE
(Yellow River)
LGIERS
Mediterranean Sea
TIBET
Heian-kyo
TUNIS
Damascus
Baghdad
CHINA
Kaifeng
Nanjing
(Kyoto)
ROCCO
Jerusalem
Delhi
Hangzhou
Medina
Punjab
Ganga River
Yangzi River
(Lin'an)
Persian
Pacific Ocean
Mecca
Gulf
MUGHAL
Nile River
EMPIRE
Red
Sea
SONGHAY
VIJAYANAGARA
Niger River
Philippines
OYO
Indian Ocean
AFRICA
Sumatra
Borneo
Mombasa
Java
Kilwa
Timor
MWENEMUTAPA
AUSTRALIA
Cape of
Good Hope

Indus River

0   2,000 mi
0   3,000 km

INTRODUCTION:
YOU ARE MAKING HISTORY!

You are looking for information about a video game you want on the Internet, and you find a perfect description on the website of the company that makes the game. The website gives you all the systems requirements and tells you all the good points about your game. It tells how many levels and scenarios there are and how highly rated the graphics are. Then you are sad to find out that its memory requirements are high and that it's sold out in stores, but you print out the information anyway, make a few notes about why it won't work, and put it aside.

A hundred years from now a writer is trying to find out what interested young people in the early 21st century, and she miraculously comes across this printout. She is ecstatic because she has found a *document*—a source that will help her figure out what young adults were doing long ago. She mentally thanks you for having preserved that record for her.

After you have looked up the video game, your parents start nagging. It's time to get serious, they say. You need to work harder and put away the video games. You need to get good grades so that you can go to college. College!? What is that anyway? You think that you have heard of one or two and go back to the trusty Internet, this time finding the website of a college. It is full of links and gorgeous pictures of students enjoying themselves. College suddenly looks a little more interesting. But some of the links are less exciting than others—such as the one on dozens of rules and regulations and another link on all the steps it takes to get into the college. You are a little put off, as you have plenty to do already. You print out some of the information about college nonetheless and write down the good points and bad points. You put it aside for some other researcher a century from now who will be looking for documents about what colleges young people were interested in way back long ago. This researcher is also happy to have a document that will help her understand what the steps were for getting into a college or university.

Without even knowing it you have preserved another primary document—a piece of information that comes right from history itself. It is precious source material that the researcher will perhaps use when she writes a book on colleges and what young people thought about them in the 21st century. Her writing will be called a "secondary source"—that is, a history written long after the events it describes, usually by looking at many documents. Primary sources are the nails and boards, glass and cement for putting together the big building we call history.

When that researcher who found your printout about the video game starts writing her history book, she will ask herself a lot of questions about that primary source. First she will want to know what's in the document—all the facts about video games. What *is* a video game, she will think to herself, and what did people do with them? Who used them? What did young people think about them? Where were they used? She will gather all the facts she can from your printout.

Then the questions become harder, more critical, and this is what all historians do; they ask the tough questions. They might ask who put out that information about the video game—or the college, for that matter. Did the person who wrote all that information have a purpose that we need to know about? We know that in the case of the websites for the video game company and the college the people who created them were trying to attract business. So behind the facts—very important in themselves—are what detectives call motives. Historians look for motives when they look at documents in a critical or questioning way.

OLD SCHOOL HISTORY

Just as our historian of the future looks at your printout to learn about 21st-century colleges, a historian today who wants to learn about early universities studies documents and records from that time period. The charters that were written to set up schools and colleges show us that for centuries universities have been communities of teachers and students formed for purposes of higher education and professional training. Students' notebooks tell us what professors said and what young people learned in their classes, and their letters home let us know about their personal and financial worries. As far back as the Middle Ages students and teachers lived together in buildings built by the church or governments. Teachers wrote rules to govern these houses, giving us an idea of what life was like for the residents. The members of the university lived and learned together under a government run by officers such as deans who enforced written regulations—some of the most important documents telling us what university life was like even at the beginning. All these documents help historians to gather the facts about early modern universities.

We learn from documents such as the founding charters and rules and regulations that as an institution the university is more than 800 years old; the earliest examples were the schools of Paris and Bologna in the 12th century. Professors founded the first of these, and students the second, but most universities were run by both students and teachers. Historians look at primary sources from each group to get a complete picture of early universities.

"Faculties" were groups of teachers involved in the teaching of the major subjects, that is, philosophy, theology (religion), law, and medicine—all subjects that helped students get jobs. The charters also tell us that undergraduates worked toward bachelor of arts degrees and perhaps master's degrees, which allowed them to teach, and some went on to doctorates in philosophy, theology, law, or medicine. "Nations" were organizations of foreign students, who otherwise would have no legal protection in the countries where they were studying. "Colleges" were student residences where teaching was carried on. Historians have figured all this out by looking at documents that are very different from the university website that you called up but that provide the same kinds of useful information.

In the 13th century, Robert of Sorbon founded a college in Paris for the teaching of theology. It is now known as the College of Sorbonne and continues to be an important university to this day. Historians have learned about the early days of the Sorbonne from its documents—written many centuries ago and kept in special files, not like the open information on the Internet. These documents, called manuscripts, were written by hand well before there was printing in Europe—or, obviously, the Internet. The many manuscript records of the Sorbonne were written in Latin and preserved in "charts"—as the original statutes or regulations were called. Among these charts are the rules Robert of Sorbon himself set down around 1274, which described and controlled the religious and domestic life and behavior of students. In his chart, Robert declared that he was only supporting "the custom that was instituted from the beginning," but he expressed these customs in particular rules that students could understand.

Our next question is: What were Robert's motives? Why did he write all these rules? We begin to think critically and ask questions about the document. We think that he must have wanted students to behave well in the big city, and he was also eager for them to contribute to the community by giving public sermons. Because these students were studying to become clergymen, they needed to show especially good behavior. We can also ask what sort of misconduct or even vandalism—including conflicts with townspeople, illegal stays in the town, or unauthorized parties—may have inspired these rules.

Robert's rules set up standards and ideals for students, limits on their behavior, and penalties for violating them. We try to see what kind of attitudes shaped rules for going to a university: Were they strict or lenient? For example, many requirements were based on biblical texts and religious customs, because in those days the university was basically a religious institution, and the professors were mainly monks or priests. Then as now, documents allow us to see that perhaps university life is about more serious things than getting away from home to a pleasant city or campus.

From these rules, we can find out as much about the daily life of students then as the Internet tells us about colleges today. They had meals in dining areas (not in their private rooms). They were required to attend religious services (no excuses). They were asked not to make "too much noise," and they were expected to take care of guests, or "outsiders," that is, pay for them, "without loss to the community." Students were required to pay professors for their lessons, but they were also allowed to criticize their teachers for inadequate performance, such as confusing lectures and useless assignments. As this was long before the age of the printed book, students had to copy their own "books" from the "lectures" (literally, readings from texts) of their professors. The students' notebooks have become primary documents, too, because they show us students and teachers in action.

YOU BE THE JUDGE

When historians look at documents they are like judges and juries trying to figure out what the truth is. They ask themselves whether a witness is reliable and whether they can believe that witness's testimony. A lot of hard thinking goes into deciding whether somebody's story is believable. Usually we trust high officials such as Robert of Sorbon, but we always check out his story—that students needed rules and regulations—with other people's stories. For instance, we might have a student's letter to his parents saying that he was following all the rules but that he needs more money because Robert of Sorbon has suddenly locked the kitchen so that he himself can have all the food. Then we'd have to think about what was really going on in this medieval university in Paris. No such letter actually exists, but we need as many documents as possible to decide which stories give us the best evidence. It takes a lot of documents to make history.

By looking at documents and figuring out what they are telling you, and whether it is true, you have learned one of the major skills not only in studying history but in making decisions and acting—that is, making history. It is amazing to think that in your everyday life you are making history all the time: when you are having fun finding and making your own documents from the

Internet, or writing letters to your friends, sending postcards from vacation, or even making a shopping list. Someone will learn a lot from your own stash of documents and stacks of printouts; they will love it that you wrote funny comments on them and that later you wrote letters (or e-mails) from college. Welcome to the world of history, which is a world of documents and sources. You yourself can make new ones and study old ones. You can ask the tough questions—be judge and jury of Robert of Sorbon or the student who writes home because Robert has locked the kitchen up. It's how we learn what humans are all about.

THE EUROPEAN WORLD, 400–1450

1. Here Come the Bad Guys

ST. JEROME, LETTER, FOURTH CENTURY

Groups of Germanic tribes that migrated into the declining Roman Empire from the north of Europe brought chaos to a troubled society. St. Jerome was one of the founding fathers of the Catholic Church, and he is especially known for his early translation of the Bible into Latin. He wrote many letters describing the events of his day to other priests. In them, he commented on the grimness of life in the fourth and early fifth centuries, and in particular on what the Romans called the barbarian invasions. These migrations of Germanic tribes helped bring about the "fall" of the Roman Empire in later generations, but they also meant misery to tens of thousands of individuals. Often refugees fleeing the invaders flocked for help to monasteries, where monks like St. Jerome gave them food and shelter. In this letter to a fellow priest, he describes the upheaval caused by the invasions and expresses his grief over the fate of the empire.

See chapters 1 and 2 of *The European World*

Innumerable and most ferocious people have overrun the whole of **Gaul.** The entire area bounded by the Alps, the **Pyrenees,** the ocean and the **Rhine** is occupied by the **Quadi, Vandals, Alammani**—O weep for the empire. . . . Mainz, once a noble city, is captured and razed, and thousands have been massacred in the church. . . . The provinces of **Aquitaine,** . . . of **Lyons** and **Narbonne** are completely occupied and devastated either by the sword from without or famine within. . . .

Gaul, modern-day France; **Pyrenees,** mountains between < France and Spain

< **Rhine,** major river in western Europe; **Quadi, Vandals, Alammani** Germanic tribes

< **Aquitaine, Lyons, Narbonne,** regions in southern and eastern France

Who would believe that Rome, victor over all the world, would fall, that she would be to her people both womb and tomb. Once all the East, Egypt and Africa acknowledged her **sway** and were counted among her menservants and her maidservants. Who would believe that holy Bethlehem would receive as beggars nobles, both men and women, once abounding in riches? Where we cannot help we mourn and mingle with theirs our tears. . . .

sway, authority >

There is not an hour, not even a moment, when we are not occupied with crowds of the **brethren**, when the peace of the monastery is not invaded by a **horde** of guests so that we shall either have to shut our gates or neglect the Scriptures for which the gates were opened.

brethren, members of the church >

horde, crowd >

Margaret Hodges retells the legend of St. Jerome and the lion he sheltered in his monastery in *St. Jerome and the Lion* (Orchard, 1991). A classic version of the same story, told in verse, is Rumer Godden's *St. Jerome and the Lion* (Viking, 1961). A scholarly edition of some of Saint Jerome's letters is published as *Selected Letters*, translated by F. A. Wright, as part of the Loeb Classical Library (Harvard University Press, 1999). *Jerome: His Life, Writings, and Controversies* by J. N. D. Kelly (Harper & Row, 1975; reprint, Henrickson, 1998) is a scholarly account of his life and works.

2. Who's the Boss?

" POPE GELASIUS I, EDICT XII, 494

See chapters 2, 5, and 9 of *The European World*

Throughout history there have been heated debates and even outright warfare over who should have final say in ruling people—a political or a religious leader.

For the entire medieval period in Europe, people fought over who should have the most power, the king or the pope. Pope Gelasius I, born in Rome to North African parents and one of the most powerful church leaders of his century, wrote a letter to the Byzantine emperor declaring that the pope was the highest authority. This letter—called an edict, or order—aroused real battles. Gelasius believed that religious leaders had the higher power because they had to answer to God for everything—including the way governments ran.

There are indeed two [powers], most **august** Emperor, by which this   < **august**, grand
world is ruled, the sacred authority of the **pontiffs** and the royal   < **pontiffs**, popes
power. Of the two the priesthood has the greater weight to the
degree that it must **render** an account for kings themselves in mat-   < **render**, give
ters divine. Know then . . . that although you **preside** with dignity in   < **preside**, rule
human affairs, as to the divine you are to submit your neck to those
from whom you look for salvation and from whom you receive the
celestial sacraments. You are to be subject rather than to rule in the   < **celestial sacraments**,
religious sphere and bow to the judgment of the priests rather than   holy rites
seek to bend them to your will. For, if in the area of public discipline
the priests recognize your authority as derived from above and obey
your laws . . . how much more willingly should you obey them who
are charged with the administration of the **venerable mysteries**? . . .   < **venerable mysteries**,
And if it is proper that the hearts of the faithful should be submitted   matters of faith, or
to priests in general, by how much more should obedience be ren-   sacred matters
dered to him who presides over that **see** which the Highest Divinity   < **see**, center of a
desired to be **preeminent** above all priests?   bishop's authority;
    preeminent, supreme

The Church by Kathryn Hinds, part of the Life in the Middle Ages
series (Benchmark, 2000) is a good overview. *The Medieval Establishment,
1200–1500,* by Geoffrey Hindley (Putnam, 1970), is a well-illustrated book
for young readers that discusses the authority of the medieval church, the
noble and merchant classes, and the influence of each on medieval society.
The Oxford Illustrated History of Christianity, by John McManners (Oxford
University Press, 1990), is a good introduction to the issues of church
authority in the medieval period and later.

3. Hagar the Horrible's Helper

ODDR SNORRASON, KING OLAF'S SAGA, ABOUT 1200

*The Vikings, who lived in what is now Scandinavia, were expert
traders, sailors, and explorers. They are known to have established
settlements in Greenland and North America and along the Baltic coast,
eventually invading England after many decades of trade with people
of that island. To accomplish all this in rough seas, they had to have
sturdy ships, and they also had to have vessels that would allow them to
defeat their enemies. The construction of the "Long Serpent" in 998 in*

> See chapter 4 of
> *The European World*

present-day Norway, one of the largest boats in the fleet, became leg-
endary, and the description was written down about two centuries later
by the Benedictine monk Oddr Snorrason, in Iceland. It tells us some-
thing about the kinds of workers involved in this huge project and about
how even the main builder had to keep a farm going.

Hladhamrar, town >
in Norway

keel, central bottom >
part of hull; 74 ells,
about 37 yards

fell, chop down >

planking, covering >
the boat's framework
with boards

The winter after King Olaf came . . . he had a great vessel built at **Hlad-**
hamrar, which was larger than any ship in the country, and of which
the frames are still to be seen there. The length of **keel** that rested
upon the grass was **seventy-four ells**. Thorberg *skafhogg* was the name
of the man in charge of making the stem and stern of the vessel; but
there were many others besides—some to **fell** wood, some to shape it,
some to make nails, some to carry timber; and all that was used was
selected very carefully. The ship was both long and broad and high-
sided, and strongly timbered. While they were **planking** the ship, it
happened that Thorberg had to go home to his farm upon some
urgent business and he remained there a long time. The ship was
planked up on both sides when he came back. That same evening the
king went out, and Thorberg with him, to see how the vessel looked,
and everybody said that never was seen so large and beautiful a ship of
war. . . . Early the next morning the king returns again to the ship, and
Thorberg with him. The carpenters were there before them, but all
were standing there and doing nothing. The king asked why they were
like that. They said that the ship was spoilt and that somebody had
gone from stem to stern, and cut one deep notch after the other down
one side of the planking. When the king came nearer he saw it was so,
and immediately said and swore that the man who had thus damaged
the ship out of envy should die if he were found out. . . . Thorberg
says, "I will tell you, king, who did it. I did it."

The king says, "You must restore it all to the same condition as
before, or your life shall pay for it."

Then Thorberg went and smoothed the ship's side until the deep
notches had all disappeared. Then the king and all present declared
that the ship was much handsomer on the side which Thorberg had
cut, and the king asked him to shape it so on both sides and gave
him great thanks for the improvements. Afterwards Thorberg was

the master-builder of the ship until she was finished. . . . The king called this ship the Long Serpent. . . . The Long Serpent had thirty-four benches for rowers. The prow and the stern were covered with gilding, and the **freeboard** was as great as in ocean-going ships. This ship was the best and most costly ship in Norway.

< freeboard, the part of the ship that is above the water

📖 *The Saga of Olaf Tryggvason / Oddr Snorrason* has been translated from the Icelandic and annotated by Theodore M. Andersson (Cornell University Press, 2003). There are many books for young readers about the Vikings and their ships, including: *The Vikings,* by Neil Grant (Oxford University Press, 1998); *The Real Vikings: Craftsmen, Traders, and Fearsome Raiders,* by Melvin Berger (National Geographic, 2003); *Viking Longboats,* by Margaret Mulvihill (Gloucester, 1989); and *The Viking Longship,* by Lynda Trent (Lucent, 1999). Some retellings of the Viking sagas for young readers include *Viking Tales,* written by Jennie Hall and illustrated by Victor R. Lamod (Rand McNally, 1930), and *Viking Tales of the North: The Sagas of Thorstein, Viking's Son, and Fridthjof the Bold,* by Rasmus Bjorn Anderson (Scott, Foresman, 1901). *Vikings: The North Atlantic Saga,* edited by William W. Fitzhugh and Elisabeth I. Ward (Smithsonian Institution Press, 2000), is the catalog of a major exhibition at the National Museum of Natural History, Smithsonian Institution.

4. Cry Babies

" LULLABY, MIDDLE AGES

This lullaby is thought to be the very first written down in the English language. A lullaby was sung to rock children to sleep. This one urges the child to think deeply about life and death, to follow the parents' teachings, and to understand God's plan for human beings. Because of a belief that life on Earth was terribly hard and full of sorrow, parents—as this lullaby shows—wanted children to know life's hard truths from a very young age. This pessimistic attitude seems to fit the turmoil of the Middle Ages, with its invasions and local fighting. In those days, too, many children did not even survive infancy because of childhood diseases, so people saw their fate as all the more bitter.

See chapter 11 of
The European World

Lollai, lollai, little child, why weepest thou so **sore**?
Needs must thou weep, it was **ordained of yore**
Ever to live in sorrow and sigh and mourn ever,

< **sore**, hard
< **ordained of yore**, destined long ago

ere, before >	As thine elders did **ere** this, while they alived were.
	Lollai, lollai, little child, child, lollai, lullow,
uncouth, harsh >	Into **uncouth** world i'comen so art thou.
	Beastes and those fowls, the fishes in the flood
i'made, is made >	And each living thing, **i'made** of bone and blood,
	When he cometh to the world he doth himself some good—
care art thou beset,	All but the wretched child that is of Adam's blood.
worries are you	Lollai, lollai, little child, by **care art thou beset**
troubled >	Thou knowest nought this **world's wild** before thee is set.
world's wild, wilder- >	Child if **betideth that thou shalt goodly be**
ness; betideth that	Think **though wert fostered** upon thy mother's knee;
thou shalt goodly be, it	Ever have mind in thy heart of those things three:
happens that you are	Whence thou comest, where thou art and what shall come
good; though wert fos-	of thee.
tered, you were raised	Lollai, lollai, little child, child, lollai, lollai.
though, you >	With sorrow **though** come into this world,
wend away, make >	With sorry shalt thou **wend away**.
your way	

Iona and Peter Opie's classic anthology, *The Oxford Book of Children's Verse* (Oxford University Press, 1973), contains a variety of medieval lullabies, prayers, and other literature for children of that period. Nicholas Orme's *Medieval Children* (Yale University Press, 2001) is a beautifully illustrated history of children's lives in England up to the 16th century. Barbara Hanawalt's *Growing up in Medieval London: The Experience of Childhood in History* (Oxford University Press, 1993) is a highly readable book about British children.

5. Piles of Heads, Hands, and Feet

❝ RAYMOND OF AGILES, EYEWITNESS ACCOUNT OF THE CAPTURE
OF JERUSALEM, 1099

See chapter 6 of
The European World

In 1095, Pope Urban II called for the leaders of Europe to band together, instead of fighting one another all the time, in a common war called a crusade. The crusade was a movement of faith and fanaticism in which Christians were encouraged to kill as many non-Christians as possible in the Middle East and elsewhere. The crusade was a political drive to capture the Holy Land (present-day Israel and surrounding territory mentioned in the Bible) from non-Christian peoples. The Europeans also hoped to profit from the riches of the Middle East, where traders exchanged Asian, African, and European goods and made fortunes. Along the way, the crusaders also slaughtered Jews, scooping up their money, too. In 1099 the crusaders, among them a knight called Raymond, took the holy city of Jerusalem after suffering defeats by the Muslim armies. Raymond left this glowing description of the Christian triumph, later published as part of a history of the Crusades.

Some of our men (and this was more merciful) cut off the heads of their enemies; others shot them with arrows, so that they fell from the towers; others tortured them longer by **casting** them into flames.   < casting, throwing
Piles of heads, hands, and feet were to be seen in the streets of the city. It was necessary to pick one's way over the bodies of men and horses. But these were small matters compared to what happened in the temple of Solomon, a place where religious services are ordinarily chanted. What happened there? If I tell the truth, it will exceed your powers of belief. So let it suffice to say this much at least, that in the temple and **portico** of Solomon, men rode in blood up to their   < portico, porch, or entranceway
knees and the bridle reins. Indeed, it was a just and splendid judgment of God, that this place should be filled with the blood of the unbelievers, when it had suffered so long from their **blasphemies.**   < blasphemies, insults to a particular religion

Now that the city was taken it was worth all our previous labors and hardships to see the devotion of the pilgrims at the **Holy Sepulchre.** . . . This day, I say, will be famous in all future ages, for it turned our labors and sorrows into joy and **exultation**; this day, I say, marks the justification of all Christianity.   < Holy Sepulchre, the chapel built where Jesus was believed to have been buried; **exultation**, celebration

A variety of documents on the Crusades can be found in *The Crusades: A Reader,* edited by S. J. Allen and Emilie Amt (Broadview, 2003). In *The Crusades through Arab Eyes* (Schocken, 1989), Amin Maalouf assembles contemporary Arab chronicles of the Crusades as well as those of eyewitnesses and often participants. For a short history of the Crusades, see *The Crusades,* by John Child (Peter Bedrick, 1996), and *Tales of the Crusades,* by Olivia E. Coolidge (Houghton Mifflin, 1970), which traces the progress of the Crusades over 300 years as experienced by many different participants. The art is based on prints by Gustave Doré. A longer history of the Crusades for adults is *The Oxford Illustrated History of the Crusades,* edited by Jonathan Riley-Smith (Oxford University Press, 1997).

6. Imagine This: A Country Is a Body

JOHN OF SALISBURY, POLICRATICUS (THE STATESMAN'S BOOK), 12TH CENTURY

See chapter 8 of
The European World

John of Salisbury was a 12th-century English bishop who had firm ideas about politics. These were especially valuable at a time when leadership was hotly contested, not just in England but across Europe. Known as a philosopher, John of Salisbury also loved and defended literature and the arts. He wrote books of advice on politics, including Policraticus, *for the rulers of his day. His advice was based on the idea that one could think about government the way one thought about the body.*

endowed with, given >

equity, justice > according to natural law

preside, rule >

venerated, honored >

quickened, inspired >

husbandmen, farmers; > cleave, cling

A commonwealth . . . is a certain body which is **endowed with** life by the benefit of divine favor, which acts at the prompting of the highest **equity**, and is ruled by what may be called the moderating power of reason. Those things which establish and implant in us the practice of religion, and transmit to us the worship of God. . . fill the place of the soul in the body of the commonwealth. And therefore those who **preside** over the practice of religion should be looked up to and **venerated** as the soul of the body. . . . The place of the head in the body of the commonwealth is filled by the prince, who is subject only to God and to those who exercise His office and represent Him on earth, even as in the human body the head is **quickened** and governed by the soul. The place of the heart is filled by the senate, from which proceeds the initiation of good works and ill. The duties of eyes, ears, and tongue are claimed by the judges and the governors of provinces. Officials and soldiers correspond to the hands. Those who always attend upon the prince are likened to the sides. Financial officers . . . may be compared with the stomach and intestines. . . . The **husbandmen** correspond to the feet, which always **cleave** to the soil, and need the more especially the care and foresight of the head, since they walk upon the earth doing service with their bodies, they meet the more often with stones and stumbling, and therefore deserve aid and protection all the more justly since it is they who raise, sustain, and move forward the weight of the entire body. . . .

Then and only then will the health of the commonwealth be sound and flourishing, when the higher members shield the lower, and the lower respond faithfully and fully in like measure to the just demands of their superiors.

📖 *The Medieval Reader*, edited by James Bruce Ross and Mary Martin McLaughlin (Penguin, 1977), contains many documents on politics and power in the Middle Ages. The complete text of John of Salisbury's *Policraticus: Of the Frivolities of Courtiers and the Footprints of Philosophers* has been edited and translated by Cary J. Nederman (Cambridge University Press, 1990). There is also an abridged edition edited by Murray F. Markland (Frederick Ungar, 1979). The *Letters* of John of Salisbury have been edited by W. J. Millor and H. E. Butler, revised by C. N. L. Brooke (Thomas Nelson, 1955–79).

7. Out of Bondage

ANONYMOUS, LOCAL RECORDS OF ANGERS, FRANCE, ABOUT 1100

In medieval Europe, a serf usually remained tied to the land for his entire life, performing duties such as serving in the master's household or working on the lord's farm. Unlike slaves, serfs could not be sold, and they had some rights, but they were not free, as we understand the word today. One way to become free was simply to run away to a city. But some serfs developed special skills while serving the lord and his community, and these could help make their lives better. This story about medieval buildings and how they were constructed and decorated was written down in the town records of Angers, France. In the story a man uses his talents to earn his freedom around the year 1100. Being freed from serfdom was so important that witnesses were to be present to certify the passage from bondage to freedom, and local officials set the story down.

See chapter 4 of
The European World

A certain man, by name Fulco, **endowed with the art** of the painter, came to the chapter of St. Aubin [of Angers, France] and there made the following agreement before the **Abbot** Girard and the whole convent: he would paint the whole monastery of theirs and whatever they should order him to do, and he would make glass windows. And thereupon he became their brother and in addition he was made a free

< **endowed with the art,** given the talent

< **abbot,** the head of a monastery, or community of monks

laymen, people who
are not members of
the clergy; cellarer,
caretaker of the
monastery's wine >

man of the abbot; and the abbot and monks gave him one acre and a half of vineyard in fee and a house, on these terms, that he should hold them in his lifetime, and after his death they should go back to the saint, unless he should have a son who would know the art of his father and hence could serve St. Aubin. At this act there were present these **laymen:** Reginald Grandis and Warin the **cellarer.**

For more information on the building of medieval cathedrals and the craftsmen who did the work, see *The Medieval Cathedral,* by William W. Lace (Lucent, 2001), and *Building the Medieval Cathedrals,* by Percy Watson (Lerner, 1979). *Life in a Medieval Village,* by Gwyneth Morgan (Lerner, 1982), describes the life and activities of serfs, farmers, and the lord and lady of the manor in a 13th-century English village. *The Cathedral Builders of the Middle Ages,* by Alain Erlande-Brandenburg and translated by Rosemary Stonehewer (Thames and Hudson/New Horizons, 1995), is a beautifully illustrated short book. *Glass-painters,* by Sarah Brown and David O'Connor (British Museum/University of Toronto Press, 1991), is a volume from the Medieval Craftsman series illustrated with many images from the collections of the British Museum.

8. You're Grounded!

See chapter 10 of
The European World

REGULATIONS FOR STUDENTS AT THE UNIVERSITY OF PARIS, 1274

Many universities were founded in Europe during the Middle Ages, when an interest in learning flourished. Some of this interest came about because of wider global contacts. Many students went to centers of learning to study religion, which helped them in their careers both in and outside the church. Robert of Sorbon—the king's chaplain after whom part of the University of Paris (the Sorbonne) is now named—created a set of rules to guide young men who lived apart from their parents while they studied. (Young women in those days usually did not gain an education outside their homes.) Some rules aimed to teach manners and to require more orderly behavior from the students while they were living among townspeople, who did not appreciate their rowdiness.

inauguration, the
formal celebration of
the beginning of
something >

I rule that the customs established by the advice of wise men at the **inauguration** of this house be observed in their entirety and in case they had been violated to date, be no longer violated.

Nobody shall eat meat during Advent (four weeks before Christmas) nor on Monday or Tuesday preceding **Lent**. . . .

As regards the fellow students who eat in their chambers, the leftovers should be collected so they would not perish and returned to the **dispenser** who will use them for the common profit of poor **clerics**. Also the students should be admonished by the house supervisor that those eating in their chambers be quiet and **refrain** from noise so that the passersby crossing the court and the street be not offended and that their fellow-students in the adjacent chambers be not disturbed in their study hours.

If a student is late for breakfast, if he comes from school or sermon or from business in service of the community he shall have his full portion; if from business of his own he will have bread only.

Also, no student shall bring friends frequently to drink at the expense of the community; if he does he has to **defray** the costs according to the estimate of the dispenser.

No student shall have the keys of the kitchen.

< **Lent**, Christian time of fasting and seeking forgiveness, from Ash Wednesday to Easter Sunday; **dispenser**, person who gives out something; **clerics**, members of the clergy; **refrain**, hold back

< **defray**, pay

Barbara A. Hanawalt's *The Middle Ages: An Illustrated History* (Oxford University Press, 1998) has considerable information about medieval universities. Another overview for young adults is *Life during the Middle Ages*, by Earle Rice (Lucent, 1998). There are several scholarly studies of medieval universities, including Alan B. Cobban's *English University Life in the Middle Ages* (Ohio State University Press, 1999), *The Medieval English Universities: Oxford and Cambridge to c. 1500* (University of California Press, 1988), Hastings Rashdall's *Universities of Europe in the Middle Ages* (Oxford University Press, 1987), and *A History of Education during the Middle Ages and the Transition to Modern Times,* by Frank Pierrepont Graves (1920; reprint, Greenwood, 1970).

9. Y'all Come

❝ EDWARD II, SUMMONS TO THE MODEL PARLIAMENT, 1295

The early 13th century was the great age of the European parliament—that is, the meeting of groups representing the people. During the movement toward parliamentary institutions such as today's United States Senate and House of Representatives, people from the

See chapter 9 of
The European World

middle classes were added to the councils of noblemen and church-men that advised the kings and helped them decide what to do. In 1295 the king of England, Edward II, issued a summons, which called the leading citizens to meet in what became known as the Model Parliament, because its form was followed by later parlia-ments. According to canon law, that is, the laws of the church, "What touches all must be approved by all"—this is the legal idea behind representative government.

Northamptonshire, a county in central England >

The king to the sheriff of **Northamptonshire**. Desiring to hold council and treat with the earls, barons, and other nobles of our realm,

perils, dangers >

as to provision against the **perils** which now threaten it, we have

Westminster, a > cathedral and religious community in London; **feast of St. Martin's**, November 11; **enjoin**, command

ordered them to meet us at **Westminster**, on the Sunday next following the **feast of St. Martin's** in the coming winter, to discuss, ordain and do whatever may be necessary to guard against this danger. We therefore firmly **enjoin** you to have chosen without delay and sent to us at the said day and place two knights from the said county and

burgesses are citizens > and a **borough** is a town granted special privileges by royal charter

two citizens from each city of the said county, and two **burgesses from each borough**, of those more discreet and powerful to achieve: in such wise that the said knights, citizens and burgesses may severally have full and sufficient power, on behalf of themselves and the community of the county, cities and boroughs to do what may then

ordained, ordered; > **writ**, a written command, particularly a command from the king for a member of Parliament to come to a meeting

be **ordained** by the common counsel . . . so that the present business may not in any way rest undone through lack of this power. And bring with you the names of the knights, citizens, and burgesses, and this **writ**. Witness the King at Canterbury, October 3.

A good history for young readers is *The Young Oxford History of Britain and Ireland*, by Kenneth O. Morgan (Oxford University Press, 1998).

10. Good Housekeeping in 1393

 MANUSCRIPT, THE GOODMAN OF PARIS, ABOUT 1393

See chapter 7 of *The European World*

People living in cities grew more prosperous in the late Middle Ages because of expanding trade and urban activity. They wanted to enjoy a comfortable life, and this demanded a lot of hard work before the invention of modern conveniences. Not only that—they wanted their family life to be pleasant. The middle-class citizen who wrote this unpublished advice book for his young wife tells her how to run the household well and how to keep him happy and healthy. The writer did this because his wife was in her late teens, much younger than he was, and had little experience in caring for a house. The husband, though, seems to know how to care for his clothes, how to clean many kinds of furniture and fabric, and how to eliminate odors and bugs.

Wherefore love your husband's person carefully, and I pray you keep him in clean **linen**, for that is your business, and because the trouble and care of outside affairs lieth with men, so must husbands take heed, and go and come, and journey hither and thither, and in rain and wind, in snow and hail, now drenched, now dry, now sweating, now shivering, ill-fed, ill-lodged, ill-warmed, and ill-bedded. And naught harmeth him, because he is upheld by the hope that he hath of the care which his wife will take of him on his return, and of the ease, the joys and the pleasures which she will do him, or cause to be done to him in her presence; to **be unshod** before a good fire, to have his feet washed and fresh shoes and **hose**, to be given good food and drink, to be well served and well looked after. . . .

< **linen**, clothes

< **be unshod**, have one's shoes off; **hose**, men's lower garment, similar to modern leggings

And in summer take heed that there be no fleas in your chamber, nor in your bed. . . . I have heard from several that if the room be strewn with alder leaves, the fleas will be caught thereon. **Item** I have heard tell that if you have at night one or two **trenchers** slimed with glue or turpentine and set about the room, with a lighted candle in the midst of each trencher, they will come and be stuck thereto. The other way that I have tried and 'tis true: take a rough cloth and spread it about your room and over your bed, and all the fleas that shall hop thereon will be caught, so that you may carry them away with the cloth. . . . I have seen blanchets [of white wool] set upon the straw and on the bed, and when the black fleas hopped thereon, they were the sooner found upon the white, and killed.

< **item**, in addition

< **trenchers**, large slabs of bread used as plates in the Middle Ages

A good collection of documents about domestic life can be found in *Women in Medieval Society,* edited by Brenda M. Bolton and others (University of Pennsylvania Press, 1976). A history of women in the period is *Uppity Women of Medieval Times,* by Vicki Leon (Conari Press, 1997).

Madeleine Pelner Cosman's *Women at Work in Medieval Europe* (Facts on File, 2000) describes the varied tasks accomplished by women in the Middle Ages. Fiona Macdonald's *Women in Medieval Times* (Peter Bedrick, 2000) gives a similar overview. *From Workshop to Warfare: The Lives of Medieval Women,* by Carol Adams and others (Cambridge University Press, 1983), and *A Small Sound of the Trumpet: Women in Medieval Life*, by Margaret Wade Labarge (Beacon, 1986), are good books about women in medieval times. A useful history is *The Lady in the Tower: Medieval Courtesy Literature for Women,* by Diane Bornstein (Archon, 1983).

There are several modern books on cooking in the Middle Ages, including Maggie Black's *The Medieval Cookbook* (Thames & Hudson, 1996) and *The Medieval Kitchen: Recipes from France and Italy,* by Odile Redon, Francoise Sabban, and Silvano Serventi (University of Chicago Press, 1998).

THE AFRICAN AND MIDDLE EASTERN WORLD, 600–1500

11. How to Catch an Elephant

AL-MAS'UDI, THE GOLDEN PLAINS, ABOUT 915

In the early modern period, the Indian Ocean was like a super-highway on which hundreds of ships carried goods to Arabs, Africans, South Asians, and Chinese. Arab ships carried a great deal of this trade, moving slaves, ivory, cotton, and other goods to many ports in the Eastern Hemisphere. One of the passengers on board a ship sailing from Oman, on the Arabian peninsula, around 915 was the traveler and historian al-Mas'udi, who visited Persia (present-day Iran), India, China, and East Africa on that particular voyage. He kept a record of his travels that was later published and then translated into French in the 19th century. In his record, al-Mas'udi described the places he visited, from city life to the food people ate, from the landscapes to what people traded. In this example, he discusses the origin of ivory traded from Africa as far as China.

See chapter 2 of *The African and Middle Eastern World*

There are many wild elephants but no tame ones. The **Zanj** do not use them for war or anything else, but only hunt and kill them. When they want to catch them, they throw down the leaves, bark and branches of a certain tree which grows in their country: then they wait in ambush until the elephants come to drink. The water burns them and makes them drunk. They fall down and cannot get up: their limbs will not **articulate**. The Zanj rush upon them armed

Zanj, Arabs' name for Africans living south of the Sahara

articulate, bend at the joints

with very long spears, and kill them for their ivory. It is from this country that come tusks weighing fifty pounds and more. They usually go to Oman, and from there are sent to China and India. This is the chief trade route, and if it were not so, ivory would be common in Muslim lands.

In China the kings and military and civil officers use ivory **palanquins**: no officer or notable dares to come into the royal presence in an iron palanquin, and ivory alone can be used. Thus they seek after straight tusks in preference to the curved, to make the things we have spoken of. They also burn ivory before their idols and **cense** their altars with it. . . . The Chinese make no other use of the elephant, and consider it unlucky to use it for domestic purposes or war. This fear has its origin in a tradition about one of their most ancient military expeditions. In India ivory is much sought after. It is used for the handles of daggers called *harari*. . . . But the chief use of ivory is making chessmen and backgammon pieces.

In the land of the Zanj the elephant lives about 400 years, according to what the people say, and they speak with certainty of having met an elephant so tall that it was impossible to kill it.

palanquins, > covered chairs on poles, carried by men or horses

cense, perfume > with smoke from burning incense

Wonders of Elephants, by Sigmund A. Lavine and Vincent Scuro (Dodd, Mead, 1979), is illustrated with photos and old prints. *African Elephants,* by Roland Smith, with photographs by Gerry Ellis (Lerner, 1995), describes the life cycle and habitats of the largest creatures in Africa. *The Life and Lore of the Elephant,* by Robert Delort (Abrams, 1992), is a color-illustrated short history with primary source documents. *Elephants: A Cultural and Natural History,* by Karl Groning (Konemann, 1999), covers the relationship between humans and elephants from the ancient world to modern times

Another medieval traveler who left accounts similar to al-Mas'udi's was Ibn Battuta. James Rumford's *Traveling Man: The Journey of Ibn Battuta, 1325–1354* (Houghton Mifflin, 2001) is a picture-book account of his journey from Morocco to China, from the steppes of Russia to the shores of Tanzania. A full biography is *The Adventures of Ibn Battuta, a Muslim Traveler of the Fourteenth Century,* by Ross E. Dunn (University of California Press, 1986). A translation of Ibn Battuta's own text has been published as *The Travels of Ibn Battuta, A.D. 1325–1354* (Cambridge University Press for the Hakluyt Society, 1958).

12. You Are My Sunshine

❝ ABU'L-TAYYIB AHMAD IBN AL-HUSAYN AL-DJU'FI AL-MUTANABBI, "PANEGYRIC TO SAIF AL-DAULA ON HIS DEPARTURE FROM ANTIOCH," MID-10TH CENTURY

When kings and princes ruled the world they were a common topic of poetry, especially when they paid the bills for the poets and singers. The writer Abu'l-Tayyib Ahmad ibn al-Husayn al-Dju'fi al-Mutanabbi began in Iraq as a poor boy, the son of a water-carrier, but he soaked up the songs and poetry of the nomadic Arab Bedouin people among whom he lived. Eventually he became the official poet of the court of the Middle Eastern ruler Saif al-Daula, and before the two had a big fight, he composed many poems to praise this ruler. These poems of praise, or panegyrics, were a kind of flashy advertisement for both the prince and the poet. In this poem, the author describes how the king's subjects—the "we" in the verses—feel when their ruler is gone.

> **Whither do you intend,** great prince? We are the herbs of
>   the hills, and you are the clouds;
> We are the ones **time has been miserly** towards respecting
>   you, and the days are cheated of your presence.
> Whether at war or at peace, you aim at the heights, whether
>   you **tarry or hasten.**
> Would that we were your **steeds** when you ride forth, and
>   your tents when you **alight!**
> Every day you load up afresh, and journey to glory, there to
>   dwell;
> and when souls are mighty, the bodies are wearied in their
>   quest.
> Even so the moons rise over us, and even so the great seas
>   are unquiet;
> And **our wont is comely patience,** were it with anything but
>   your absence that we were tried.
> Every life you do not grace is death; every sun that you are
>   not is darkness
> . . . .
> The awe inspired in our hearts by Saif al-Daula the king, the
>   object of our hopes, is itself a sword,

> See chapter 5 of *The African and Middle Eastern World*

Whither do you intend, where are you going

time has been miserly, in this line, the author is saying that the people miss the prince

tarry or hasten, take your time or hurry

alight, dismount, or get off one's horse, or steed

our wont is comely patience, in this line the author is saying that the people are usually patient except when they are waiting for their king shun, avoid > So it is much for the brave to **shun** him, and it is much for the eloquent to speak a greeting.

> *The Bedouins*, by Olga Hoyt (Lothrop, Lee & Shepard, 1969), describes the customs, religion, wars, and way of life of the Bedouins of Arabia. Thierry Mauger's *The Ark of the Desert* (Souffles, 1991) describes the social life and customs of the Bedouins of Saudi Arabia. *Antioch: The Lost Ancient City* (Princeton University Press, 2000), edited by Christine Kondoleon, is the catalog of an exhibition at the Worcester Art Museum.

13. Tourist Guide to Ghana

ABU 'UBAYD 'ABD ALLAH BIN 'ABD AL-'AZIZ AL-BAKRI, THE BOOK OF ROUTES AND REALMS, 11TH CENTURY

See chapters 5, 9, and 10 of *The African and Middle Eastern World*

Ghana, in West Africa, was one of the booming kingdoms of the medieval and early modern period. Over several centuries its people carried out a brisk trade in gold, slaves, and other goods. The resulting prosperity allowed the people of Ghana to build handsome buildings and attractive cities; Ghana's rulers lived in splendor, leading their people in a variety of ceremonies and festivals. So renowned was the kingdom that travelers made sure to visit it on their travels around the Mediterranean and Africa, and they brought back many reports or simply recorded their observations of geography and the ways people lived.

One of the great writers on Africa is Abu 'Ubayd 'Abd Allah bin 'Abd al-'Aziz al-Bakri, commonly known as al-Bakri. He lived in Spain in the 11th century when it was under Muslim rule, and he wrote learned works on many subjects, among them geography. His book of geography called The Book of Routes and Realms *reads like a vivid account of a personal tour. Al-Bakri, however, never left Spain, even though his work is considered to be among the most accurate of all the descriptive books of its day. Instead, he compiled his descriptions from numerous other sources, such as the accounts of other travelers, creating a narrative that still serves as a helpful guide to the Africa of a thousand years ago.*

city of Ghana, Ghana's royal central city, which archaeologists have not yet found >

The **city of Ghana** consists of two towns situated on a plain. One of these towns, which is inhabited by Muslims, is large and possesses twelve mosques, in one of which they assemble for the Friday prayer. There are salaried **imams and muezzins**, as well as **jurists** and scholars. In the environs are wells with sweet water, from which they drink and with which they grow vegetables. The king's town is six miles distant from this one and bears the name of Al-Ghaba. Between these two towns there are **continuous habitations**. The houses of the inhabitants are of stone and acacia wood. The king has a palace, a number of domed dwellings all surrounded with an enclosure like a city wall. In the king's town, and not far from his court of justice, is a mosque where the Muslims who arrive at his court pray. Around the king's town are domed buildings and groves and thickets where the sorcerers of these people, men in charge of the religious cult, live. In them too are the idols and the tombs of their kings. These woods are guarded and none may enter them and know what is there. In them also are the king's prisons. If somebody is imprisoned there, no news of him is ever heard. The king's interpreters, the official in charge of his treasury, and the majority of his ministers are Muslims. Among the people who follow the king's religion, only he and his heir apparent (who is the son of his sister) may wear **sewn clothes**. All other people wear robes of cotton, silk, or brocade, according to their means. All of them shave their beards, and women shave their heads.

< **imams and muezzins,** Islamic leaders and criers who call Muslims to prayer; **jurist,** someone with a thorough knowledge of the law, such as a judge; **continuous habitations,** the area between the two cities is filled with houses

< **sewn clothes,** that is, the other people just wrap cloth around themselves

This account comes from an anthology entitled *Corpus of Early Arabic Sources for West African History,* edited and translated by J. F. P. Hopkins and N. Levtzion (Cambridge University Press, 1981). A good short history of Arab geography is Pier Giovanni Donini's *Arab Travelers and Geographers* (Immel, 1991). *Ancient Ghana: The Land of Gold,* by Philip Koslow (Chelsea House, 1995); *Ghana, Mali, Songhay: The Western Sudan,* by Kenny Mann (Dillon Press, 1996); and *The Royal Kingdoms of Ghana, Mali, and Songhay: Life in Medieval Africa,* by Patricia and Fredrick McKissack (Henry Holt, 1994), are useful histories for young readers.

14. Balcony over Troubled Waters

" USAMA IBN MUNQIDH, MEMOIRS, 12TH CENTURY

See chapter 5 of *The African and Middle Eastern World*

Usama ibn Munqidh, who was born at the end of the 11th century, lived in troubled times. In his homeland, part of the Holy Land that is in modern-day Syria, he experienced at first hand the arrival of crusaders from France. Simultaneously, his country was overrun by local warring factions struggling for control of the region. Usama ibn Munqidh kept a remarkable diary of his family's existence during these difficult days and recorded his dealings with the Franks, as he called the Europeans. These invaders he found particularly ignorant, even barbarian, though he dealt with them every day when some of them settled nearby. He also recorded how his family coped with the various invasions by competing groups of Muslims. In this passage he describes how his mother protected her daughter from capture when a group of Shi'ite Muslims (members of one of the two major branches of the Islamic faith) invaded in hope of seizing political control.

Allah, the Islamic > name for God; **quilted jerkins**, thick, close-fitting jackets

Usama's mother as a warrior.—On that day my mother (may **Allah** have mercy upon her soul!) distributed my swords and **quilted jerkins**. She came to a sister of mine who was well advanced in years and said, "Put on thy shoes and thy wrapper." This she did. My mother then led her to the balcony in my house overlooking the valley from the east. She made her take a seat there, and my mother herself sat at the entrance to the balcony. Allah (praise be to him!) gave victory over the enemy. I then came to my house seeking some of my weapons, but found noth-

scabbards, sheaths, > or cases

ing except the **scabbards** of the swords and the leather bags of the jerkins. I said, "O mother, where are my arms?" She replied, "My dear son, I have given the arms to those who would fight on our behalf, not believing that thou wert still alive." I said, "And my sister, what is she doing here?" She replied, "O my dear son, I have given her a seat at the balcony and sat behind her so that in case I found that the Batinites [the enemy] had reached us, I could push her and throw her into the valley, preferring to see her dead rather than to see her captive in the hands of the peasants. . . ." I thanked my mother for her deed and so did my sis-

solicitude, care, thoughtfulness >

ter, who prayed that mother be rewarded [by Allah] in her behalf. Such **solicitude** for honor is indeed stronger than the solicitude of men.

In *The Crusades through Arab Eyes* (Schocken, 1989), Amin Maalouf brings together contemporary Arab chronicles of the Crusades as well as those of eyewitnesses and often participants. For a short history of the Crusades, see *The Crusades,* by John Child (Peter Bedrick, 1996), and *Tales of the Crusades,* by Olivia E. Coolidge (Houghton Mifflin, 1970), which traces the progress of the Crusades over 300 years as experienced by many different participants. The art is based on prints by Gustave Dore. A longer history of the Crusades for adults is *The Oxford Illustrated History of the Crusades,* edited by Jonathan Riley-Smith (Oxford University Press, 1997).

15. Hot and Bothered in the 12th Century

ABU 'ABD ALLAH MUHAMMAD AL-SHARIF AL-IDRISI, THE PLEASURE OF HIM WHO LONGS TO CROSS THE HORIZONS, 1154

For traders, crossing the Sahara Desert was a major undertaking, but a very profitable one. Caravans carried gold, slaves, salt, and other items for sale. Abu 'Abd Allah Muhammad al-sharif al-Idrisi is thought to have been a Moroccan from North Africa. He was a traveler who later wrote accurate books of geography that were helpful to people making journeys. His books not only included maps and descriptions of the countryside, but also gave tips on local customs and food. For example, in the Sudan, in Africa, people found huge truffles—valuable mushrooms—and cooked them with their camel meat for dinner. But perhaps the most important information that al-Idrisi provided was about how to make the dangerous trip across the desert in order to see the sights of the wealthy African kingdoms and to make money in trade.

> See chapters 9 and 10 of *The African and Middle Eastern World*

This desert is crossed by travelers in the autumn. They travel in the following manner: they load their camels at late dawn, and march until the sun has risen, its light has become bright in the air, and the heat on the ground has become severe. Then they put their loads down, **hobble** their camels, unfasten their baggage and stretch awnings to give some shade from the scorching heat and the hot winds of midday. They remain thus until the beginning of the late afternoon. When the sun begins to decline and sink in the west, they set off. They march for the

< **hobble,** tie an animal's legs together to prevent it from straying

rest of the day, and keep going till nightfall, when they encamp at whatever place they have reached. They pass the rest of the night there until
late dawn, when they depart. Thus the traveling of the merchants who
enter the country of the Sudan is according to this pattern. They do not
deviate from it, because the sun kills with its heat those who run the
risk of marching at midday, when the heat is intense and the ground
is scorched. For this reason they **adhere** to the manner of traveling
described above.

deviate, depart from >

adhere, stick to >

The only English edition of al-Idrisi's writings is *India and the Neighboring Territories, as Described by the Sharif al-Idrisi in his Kitab Nuzhat al-mushtaq fi 'khtiraq al-'af-aq* (Department of Arabic and Islamic Studies, Muslim University, 1954). The excerpt printed here comes from the anthology *Corpus of Early Arabic Sources for West African History,* edited and translated by J. F. P. Hopkins and N. Levtzion (Cambridge University Press, 1981). *Sahara: Vanishing Cultures,* by Jan Reynolds (Harcourt Brace Jovanovich, 1991), describes the Tuareg people and the environment of the Sahara region in modern times.

Sahara, by Michael Palin (Thomas Dunne Books/St. Martin's Press, 2003), is the account of a modern traveler in the desert. *The Sahara,* by Jeremy Swift and the editors of Time-Life Books (Time-Life Books, 1975), is a good illustrated description of the region.

16. A Loaf of Bread

OMAR KHAYYAM, RUBAIYAT, ABOUT 1100

See chapter 6 of *The African and Middle Eastern World*

Sufism developed as a form of Islam from the eighth century on, and spread, along with Islam itself, to many parts of the world. Sufism emphasized inner devotion, an intense quest after union with God, and rejection of the material world. Sometimes Sufis (those who practice Sufism) used the word "intoxication" to describe their intense spiritual happiness and used poetry, dance, and music as expressions of their worship. Sufis also wrote about especially deep love, and their verses often sound like poetry describing love between men and women. For Sufis, however, this love poetry referred to the love of God and was very religious. The Persian mathematician and scientist Omar Khayyam wrote his book of poems, Rubaiyat *("Quatrains," groups of four lines of verse), around 1100. When they were translated into English in the 19th century, his verses became some of the world's best-known poetry. These three quatrains, like the* Rubaiyat *as a whole, are concerned with nature and the quickness of life's passing.*

Each morn a thousand Roses brings, you say;
Yes, but where leaves the Rose of Yesterday?
And this first Summer month that brings the Rose
Shall take **Jamshýd and Kaikobád** away.

<Jamshýd and Kaikobád Persian kings

A Book of Verses underneath the Bough,
A Jug of Wine, a Loaf of Bread—and Thou
Beside me singing in the Wilderness—
Oh, Wilderness were Paradise **enow**!

<enow, enough

The Worldly Hope men set their Hearts upon
Turns Ashes—or it prospers; and **anon**,
Like Snow upon the Desert's dusty Face,
Lighting a little hour or two—is gone.

<anon, soon

A classic 19th-century translation of *The Rubaiyat of Omar Khayyam* is by Edward FitzGerald (Running Press, 1989; Dover Publications, 1990); a critical edition of that translation is by Christopher Decker (University Press of Virginia, 1997). A newer translation is by Peter Avery and John Heath-Stubbs (Penguin, 1979).

17. Bright Lights, Big City

BENJAMIN OF TUDELA, TRAVELS, ABOUT 1174

In 1160 the rabbi Benjamin of Tudela in Navarre in northern Spain set out on a trip through the eastern Mediterranean and into Persia and Mesopotamia (present-day Iran and Iraq). He observed the living situation of the Jews along his route but also passed on a general account of the cities he visited—around 300 of them. In Constantinople, modern-day Istanbul, Turkey, he found a wealthy hub of trade and other activity. He described the many attractions of the city and its people, especially the deep, sometimes difficult connections among Muslim, European Christian, and Jewish inhabitants. The Crusades had taught Europeans that there was much to learn from the Middle East, including principles of architecture that would influence the construction of castles and cathedrals. When Benjamin returned to

See chapters 2 and 8 of *The African and Middle Eastern World*

Navarre in 1173, he published this account of his travels in Hebrew. Others soon translated it into several languages because its description of everyday life was so full, vivid, and reliable.

The circumference of the city of Constantinople is eighteen miles. . . . Great **stir and bustle** prevails at Constantinople in consequence of the **conflux** of many merchants, who **resort thither**, by land and by sea, from all parts of the world for purposes of trade. In this respect the city is equaled only by Baghdad, the metropolis of the **Mohammedans**. At Constantinople is the place of worship called St. Sophia, and the metropolitan seat of the pope of the Greeks, who are **at variance** with the pope of Rome. It contains as many altars as there are days of the year, and possesses innumerable riches, which are **augmented** every year by the contributions of the **two islands** and of the adjacent towns and villages. All the other places of worship in the whole world do not equal St. Sophia in riches. . . . The Hippodrome is a public place near the wall of the palace, set aside for the king's sports. Every year the birthday of Jesus the **Nazarene** is celebrated there with public rejoicings. On these occasions you may see there representations of all the nations who inhabit the different parts of the world, with surprising feats of **jugglery**. . . .

The tribute which is brought to Constantinople every year from all parts of Greece, consisting of silks and purple cloths and gold, fills many towers. These riches and buildings are equaled nowhere in the world. . . . The number of Jews at Constantinople amounts to [2,500], who live in one spot, but divided by a wall. . . . Many of them are manufacturers of silk cloths, many others are merchants, some being extremely rich; but no Jew is allowed to ride upon a horse except R. Solomon Hamritsri, who is the king's physician, and by whose influence the Jews enjoy many advantages, even in their state of oppression, which is very severely felt by them.

stir and bustle > activity; **conflux,** meeting; **resort thither,** come there

Mohammedans, > Muslims

at variance, disagree >

augmented, added to >

two islands, two of > the eight islands near Constantinople, today called Princes' Islands

Nazarene, > from Nazareth, the city in present-day northern Israel where Jesus was born; **jugglery,** acrobatics, juggling, and other circus-type acts

The full book by Benjamin of Tudela is published as *The Itinerary of Benjamin of Tudela: Travels in the Middle Ages* (Nightingale Resources, 1983, and also by J. Simon, 1983). A newer edition is *The Travels of Benjamin of Tudela: Through Three Continents in the Twelfth Century,* by Uri

Shulevitz (Farrar, Straus & Giroux, 2005). *The World of Benjamin of Tudela: A Medieval Mediterranean Travelogue,* by Sandra Benjamin (Fairleigh Dickinson University Press, 1995), is a scholarly biography. Isaac Asimov's *Constantinople: The Forgotten Empire* (Houghton Mifflin, 1970) is an accessible history of Constantinople and the Byzantine Empire from the 11th through the 15th centuries.

18. Mountain of Stone

❝ ORAL LEGEND OF SUNDIATA, 13TH CENTURY

History that is spoken, sung, or performed like a play or television show has been common among many different peoples. Spoken stories today are called legends, myths, or epics. In West Africa, one of the most important legends is about the hero Sundiata Keita, who fought a king named Sumanguru and defeated him about 1240. The griots, performers who tell or sing stories about African history, use the triumph of Sundiata to explain the founding of the magnificent kingdom of Mali, which succeeded Ghana as a leading African state. This version of the Sundiata legend was written down from versions that are still sung or told today all over West Africa.

> See chapters 1 and 10 of *The African and Middle Eastern World*

As Sundiata advanced with his army to meet Sumanguru, he learned that Sumanguru was also coming against him with an army prepared for battle. They met in a place called **Kirina**. When Sundiata turned his eyes on the army of Sumanguru he believed they were a cloud and said, "What is this cloud on the eastern side?" They told him it was the army of Sumanguru. As for Sumanguru, when he saw the army of Sundiata, he exclaimed: "What is that mountain of stone?" For he thought it was a mountain. And they told him: "It is the army of Sundiata, which lies to the west of us." Then the two columns came together and fought a murderous battle; in the thick of the fight, Sundiata uttered a great shout in the face of the warriors of Sumanguru, and at once these ran to get behind Sumanguru; the latter in his **return** uttered a great shout in the face of the warriors of Sundiata, all of whom fled to get behind Sundiata. Usually, when Sumanguru shouted, eight heads would **rise above** his own head.

< **Kirina**, somewhere in West Africa

< **return**, reply

< **rise above**, show themselves, as a way of demonstrating support

Sangaran Danguinia > **Konnte**, one of Sundiata's warriors; **taboo**, something forbidden; in this case, a prophecy that Sumanguru would soon be defeated in battle

When they had done this, Sundiata said to **Sangaran Danguinia Konnte**: "Have you forgotten the **taboo**?" As soon as Sangaran Danguinia heard of Sundiata's question he came to the front of the army, halted, grasped the arrow armed with the spur of a white cock, and threw it at Sumanguru. As soon as it had struck Sumanguru, Sangaran said: "This is the arrow of him who knows the ancient secrets. . . ." While he was saying this, Sumanguru vanished and was seen no more. Now he had had a gold bracelet on his wrist, and this fell on that spot [Kirina]; a **baobab** tree grew out of it and carries the mark to this day.

baobab, an African > tree with a very thick trunk and large edible fruit

Susu, West > African people

As for Sundiata, he defeated the army of Sumanguru, ravaged the land of the **Susu** and subjugated its people. Afterwards Sundiata became the ruler of an immense empire.

📖 *Sundiata: The Epic of the Lion King,* by Roland Bertol (Thomas Y. Crowell, 1970), is a retelling of the African epic in which a disabled child grows up to become the liberator and founder of the great empire of Mali. *Sundiata: A Legend of Africa,* by Will Eisner (NBM, 2002), is a more recent adaptation of these West African folk tales in comic-strip style. *Sundiata: An Epic of Old Mali,* by Djibril Tamsir Niane (Longman, 1965), and *Sundiata: Lion King of Mali,* written and illustrated by David Wisniewski (Clarion, 1992), are two other versions.

19. A Guide for New Muslims in India

❝ MUHAMMAD MUJIR WAJIB ADIB, THE KEY TO PARADISE, AROUND 1350

See chapters 6 and 8 of *The African and Middle Eastern World* and chapter 8 of *The Asian World*

Muslim warriors, missionaries, and traders helped spread Islam around the world from the time of the prophet Muhammad. Islam spread in particular force to Africa and Central and South Asia. Religious leaders then wrote guides for converts to Islam to help them perform their religious duties faithfully and effectively. The Key to Paradise, an advice book for new converts in India, appeared sometime in the 1350s. Its author was Muhammad Mujir Wajib Adib, who trained with a Sufi leader in Delhi, India. Sufism, a form of Islam that emphasizes a strong inner faith, continues to attract millions of followers. Like other guides to Islam, The Key to Paradise tells of the rituals that good Muslims need to follow, the kind of charity they should practice, and the values they should hold.

On Remembering God:

It is reported that a man came to the **Prophet** and said, "O Prophet of God, the obligations of Islam are many. Advise me a little of what I should do, in the letter and in the spirit." The Prophet said, "Keep your lips moist by repeating God's name."

< **Prophet,** Muhammad, the founder of Islam

On the Excellence of Reading the **Qur'an:** It is set down that the servant of God should make the Qur'an his guide and his protection. On the **Day of Judgment** the Qur'an will precede him and lead him toward Paradise. Whoever does not **diligently** stay close to the Qur'an but lags behind, the angel will come forth and striking him on his side will carry him off to hell. . . .

< **Qur'an,** the main holy scripture of Islam

< **Day of Judgment,** time of great upheaval, or the end of the world; **diligently,** carefully

It is reported in tradition that one's rank in Paradise depends upon the extent of one's recitation of the Qur'an. They say that everyone who knows how to read a small amount of the Qur'an will enjoy a high position in Paradise and they say the more one knows how to read it, the higher one's status in Paradise. Utba ibn 'Amr says that he heard the Prophet say, "Whoever reads the Qur'an in secret is the same kind of person who gives **alms** in secret, and whoever reads the Qur'an openly is like him who gives alms openly." The Prophet said that on the night of his **ascent** to heaven he was shown the sins of his people. He did not see any greater sin that that of him who did not know and did not read the Qur'an.

< **alms,** aid, such as money or food, given to the poor; **ascent,** rising

Some modern equivalents of this guide are *A Muslim Primer: Beginner's Guide to Islam,* by Ira G. Zepp (University of Arkansas Press, 2000); *The Everything Understanding Islam Book: A Complete and Easy-to-Read Guide to Muslim Beliefs, Practices, Traditions, and Culture,* by Christine Huda Dodge (Adams Media Corp., 2003); and *Islam, a Guide for Jews and Christians,* by F. E. Peters (Princeton University Press, 2003).

20. Singing, Swinging History

❝ ORAL HISTORY, NO DATE

In West Africa a griot is someone who tells, sings, or otherwise performs the tales of kings and great people of African history, as well as family genealogies. This kind of history told by singing or

See chapters 10 and 11 of *The African and Middle Eastern World reciting is known as oral history or the oral tradition. The griot used his knowledge of history to advise kings. Griots got their training from other members of their family, for as with other great professions and crafts of the early modern period, parents handed down knowledge just as schools have come to do today. So how did these words from a griot get written down? Sixty or more years ago a French scholar of African history met a griot named Djeli Mamadou Kouyate, who introduced his history with a description of his great abilities. We think that this performance as it was written down was probably similar to the words of Kouyate's griot ancestors centuries ago—although the musical part of the performance is missing.*

Keita princes of Mali, Sundiata Keita's royal line of rulers >

repositories, storage > places

vanish into oblivion, > be forgotten

savanna, grassy > plains with few trees

I am a griot. It is I, Djeli Mamadou Kouyate, son of Bintou Kouyate and Djeli Kediane Kouyate, master in the art of eloquence. Since time immemorial the Kouyates have been in the service of the **Keita princes of Mali**; we are vessels of speech, we are the **repositories** which harbor secrets many centuries old. The art of eloquence has no secrets for us; without us the names of kings would **vanish into oblivion**, we are the memory of mankind; by the spoken word we bring to life the deeds and exploits of kings for younger generations. . . . I know the list of all the sovereigns who succeeded to the throne of Mali. . . . I teach kings the history of their ancestors so that the lives of the ancients might serve them as an example, for the world is old, but the future springs from the past. . . . Listen to my word, you who want to know; by my mouth you will learn the history of Mali. . . . Listen then, sons of Mali, children of the black people, listen to my word, for I am going to tell you of Sundiata, the father of the Bright Country, of the **savanna** land, the ancestor of those who draw the bow, the master of a hundred vanished kings.

Griots and Griottes: Masters of Words and Music, by Thomas A. Hale (Indiana University Press, 1999), is an accessible overview of the functions and music of griots throughout history. *In Griot Time: An American Guitarist in Mali,* by Banning Eyre (Temple University Press, 2000), is a modern description of the griot musicians of Mali and how ancient traditions meet the modern entertainment industry. *The Griot Sings* is a collection of African songs in English translation, set to music, collected and adapted by Edna Smith (Medgar Evers College Press, 1978).

21. Who Did What in Africa

" **MAHMUD KATI, TARIKH AL-FETTASH, EARLY 16TH CENTURY**

In the 15th and 16th centuries, there resided in Timbuktu, in what is now Mali, a scholar named Mahmud Kati, who is said to have lived for 125 years. Timbuktu was full of very smart and studious people, and it was known as a center for the study of Islam, the law, and literature. Mahmud Kati knew a great deal and was thus an adviser to the powerful emperor Askia Muhammad, who ruled from 1493 to 1529. While spending a lot of time with Askia Muhammad, he began writing the story of the kingdom, including the way the society worked. Manuscripts written in Timbuktu, such as that of Mahmud Kati, were said to be the most costly goods sold in the African trade of the time, earning higher prices than gold or slaves.

Here he tells about the duties of various tribes that Askia Muhammad ruled. He describes a social system very much like the strict caste system of India and the feudal system of Europe. In all three societies, an individual was born into a group that was dedicated to a certain job. For example, according to the Hindu tradition of India, the members of the highest caste (or group), the Brahman, are the priests; in the feudal system, members of the lowest class, called serfs, did the agricultural work.

See chapter 10 of
*The African and
Middle Eastern World*

Three of these [**vassal** tribes] were from the **pagan** peoples of Bambara. . . . These tribes had in fact become vassals of the king of Mali at a time when the latter was of great power, and after having themselves previously enjoyed authority over the king of Mali. . . . They became domestic serfs of the king of Mali. . . .

vassal, a person, or in this case a tribe, that owes allegiance to another person or tribe; **pagan**, following a religion other than Islam, Christianity, or Judaism

Bambara, a large group living along the coast of West Africa

The fourth of these tribes was called **Tyindiketa**. . . . Their service . . . was to cut fodder [food] for the horses. . . .

Tyindiketa, a group of African people

The fifth was that of the **Zanj.** Each Zanj from the **Kanta** to the **Dibiridugu** owed a duty that was exacted every year at the time of low water on the river. It consisted in ten packets of dried fish for those who could provide it [or less for those who could not]. . . . And every time the prince was asked for river transport, he provided it from the canoes of this tribe, together with a crew. . . .

Zanj, a term applied by Arabs to Africans living south of the Sahara; **Kanta, Dibiridugu**, names for groups of African people

The sixth tribe were called **Arbi.** They were the personal servants and escorts of the prince. . . .

Arbi, a group of African people

tributes, groups>
owing service

As for the seventh, eighth, ninth, tenth and eleventh **tributes**, who were blacksmiths, they owed a duty of one hundred spears and one hundred arrows every year for each family of them.

Oral Epics from Africa: Vibrant Voices from a Vast Continent, edited by John William Johnson, Thomas A. Hale, and Stephen Belcher (Indiana University Press, 1997), includes a short chapter, "The Epic of Askia Mohammed," as well as many other African epics. *The Epic of Askia Mohammed,* recorded, translated, edited, and annotated by Thomas A. Hale and recounted by Nouhou Malio with the assistance of Mounkaila Maiga (Indiana University Press, 1996), is a longer version. *Scribe, Griot, and Novelist: Narrative Interpreters of the Songhay Empire,* also by Thomas A. Hale (University of Florida Press, 1990), includes "The Epic of Askia Mohammed," recounted by Nouhou Malio.

There are several histories of Mali for young readers: *Ghana, Mali, Songhay: The Western Sudan* by Kenny Mann (Dillon Press, 1996), *Mali: Crossroads of Africa* by Philip Koslow (Chelsea House, 1995), and *The Royal Kingdoms of Ghana, Mali, and Songhay: Life in Medieval Africa* by Patricia and Fredrick McKissack (Henry Holt, 1994). *Mali,* by Allan Carpenter, Thomas O'Toole, and Mark LaPointe (Childrens Press, 1975), covers the modern country of Mali. *A Glorious Age in Africa: The Story of Three Great African Empires,* by Daniel Chu (1963; reprint, Africa World Press, 1990), tells the history of the empires of Mali, Ghana, and Songhay. A classic title, *Great Rulers of the African Past,* by Lavinia G. Dobler (Doubleday, 1965), relates the history of Africa from the 13th to the 17th centuries through the lives of five of its rulers, including Mansa Musa and Askia Muhammad.

THE ASIAN WORLD, 600–1500

22. Eat Your Veggies!

❝ LANKAVATARA SUTRA, ABOUT FIFTH CENTURY

Hindu and Buddhist religious thinkers of South Asia believed in the idea of the interconnectedness of all life. Many of them also believed in reincarnation—the notion that the soul was reborn after death into another body, possibly human but just as likely that of an animal. Reincarnation continued over centuries until the soul finally became so perfect that the process of rebirth stopped. This meant that humans and animals were intimately related to one another. Some groups of Buddhists allowed eating meat as long as the animal was not raised solely for the purpose of food, but other groups strongly objected to eating any animals. They followed the advice in the traditional holy writing of the Lankavatara Sutra, which Buddhists believed to be the direct words of the Buddha, the founder of their faith.

We don't know exactly when his words were written down, or by whom, but some people believe that Hui-k'e, the Buddha's main follower, received the sutra directly from the Buddha. The full name of this sutra (which means "thread") is Saddharma-lankavatara-sutra, Sanskrit for "sutra of the appearance of good doctrine in Lanka." Lanka is a mythical city, and the name of the sutra probably means that the Buddha spoke the "good doctrine," his teachings, there.

See chapter 1 of *The Asian World*

Here in this long journey of birth-and-death there is no living being who . . . has not at some time been your mother or father, brother or sister, son or daughter. . . . So how can the **bodhisattva**, who wishes to treat all beings as though they were himself, . . . eat the flesh of

bodhisattva, enlightened being who delays achieving perfection in < order to help others any living being? Therefore, wherever living beings evolve, men should feel toward them as to their own kin, and looking on all beings as their only child, should refrain from eating meat.

The bodhisattva, . . . desirous of cultivating the virtue of love, should not eat meat, lest he cause terror to living beings. Dogs, when they see, even at a distance, an **outcaste** . . . who likes eating meat, are terrified with fear, and think, "They are the dealers of death, they will kill us!" Even the **animalculae** in earth and air and water, who have a very keen sense of smell, will detect at a distance the odor of the demons in meat-eaters, and will run away as fast as they can from the death which threatens them. . . .

> **outcaste**, person of very low social status

> **animalculae**, microscopic living things such as bacteria

Pressed by a desire for the taste of meat, people may string together their **sophistries** in defense of meat-eating . . . and declare that **the Lord** permitted meat as legitimate food, that it occurs in the list of permitted foods, and that he himself ate it. But . . . it is nowhere allowed in the **sutras** as a . . . legitimate food. . . . All meat-eating in any form or manner and in any circumstances is prohibited, unconditionally and once and for all.

> **sophistries**, subtle or crafty reasoning; **the Lord**, the Buddha

> **sutras**, Hindu or Buddhist sacred writings

This excerpt from the Lakavatara Sutra comes from *Sources of Indian Tradition,* an anthology edited by William Theodore deBary (Columbia University Press, 1958). The full text of the Lankavatara Sutra has been translated from the original Sanskrit by Daisetz Teitaro Suzuki (Routledge & Kegan Paul, 1973). *The Buddha,* by F. W. Rawding (Lerner, 1979), is a useful biography for young readers. *Buddhism,* by John Snelling (Bookwright, 1986), gives an overview of the religion.

Colin Spencer's *The Heretic's Feast: A History of Vegetarianism* (University Press of New England, 1995) and his *Vegetarianism: A History* (Four Walls Eight Windows, 2002) are histories of vegetarianism in all cultures.

23. On the Road

HUILI, THE LIFE OF XUANZANG, SEVENTH CENTURY

See chapter 2 of
The Asian World

In China in 629 CE, during the reign of the great Tang dynasty emperor Taizong, the Buddhist monk Xuanzang began a journey across China, through Central Asia, and into India in order to consult sacred documents and to learn from the leading Buddhist thinkers.

Xuanzang was 27 years old when he set out and 42 when he returned. His journey of more than 10,000 miles through some of the most rugged territory in the world was full of peril. It was a journey that connected the various regions and peoples of Asia, as Xuanzang carried with him news and ideas. The story of his exhausting trip spread, making him a legend in his own time. The Tang emperor had refused him permission to make the journey and even sent soldiers to prevent him from leaving the country, but upon Xuanzang's return in 645 Taizong was so deeply impressed by his subject's devotion and wisdom that he made Buddhism a favored religion in his country. Travelers like Xuanzang carried ideas and beliefs across deserts, mountain ranges, and the borders of empires.

Xuanzang's disciple and assistant, Huili, wrote this version of the monk's story during his lifetime. The saga includes accounts of Xuanzang's struggles and the many dangers he faced. The story of Xuanzang's journey has been retold in many different forms among many Asian peoples—much as the tales of King Arthur have been told in Europe.

Time seems to stop. In utter despair he [Xuanzang] begins to trace his steps back toward China and the **fourth watchtower.** Then he remembers his oath that he would rather die with his face toward the west than return and live in the east. Again he sets off. For four days and five nights the pilgrim and his horse struggle westward. Not a drop of water anywhere. His mouth, lips, and throat are parched by the burning heat. The evening of the fifth day the horse and rider fall down exhausted.

> **fourth watchtower,** the fourth in a series of watchtowers guarding the borders of the empire

Xuanzang collapses on the sand. He prays to the Compassionate One **Guanyin.** Dew falls on the pilgrim and his horse. He is able to slide into a deep slumber. He dreams of a tall spirit who calls out to him, "Why do you sleep instead of going forward with **zeal?**"

> **Guanyin,** Chinese Buddhist goddess of mercy; **zeal,** compassion

Once more he sets forth with his skinny **roan** horse. He has gone nearly four miles when suddenly the horse starts off in a different direction. He lets himself be guided by the creature's instincts. Soon Xuanzang catches sight of a green oasis. In it is a shining pool as bright as a mirror. The pilgrim drinks long and deep. He refills his water bag with the water of life. He and his horse rest for a day before going on. Xuanzang reaches his destination, the oasis of Hami, on the other side of the **Taklamakan Desert.**

> **roan,** horse with a finely speckled coat

> **Taklamakan Desert,** arid region in western China

A few days later the monk encounters more dangers.

No warning. It had been a spring day like any other. Xuanzang and his **entourage** descend from the **vale of Kashmir** to find their way down to the great . . . **Gangetic plain** of north India. The setting is a forest . . . fifty robbers are lying in wait for just such a caravan. They ambush the pilgrim and his party, strip them of their clothes, steal their goods, and chase them into a dried-up marsh. The former lake, enclosed by a wall of matted vines and thorns, makes an ideal pen for slaughter. The **brigands** are already beginning to tie up some caravan members when a young monk helps Xuanzang escape. The two of them get away and seek help from a village a mile away. The rescuers from the village free those who had been tied up. Everyone is shaken by the loss of their possessions and their narrow escape from death. Xuanzang alone seems untouched by what had happened. "Life is the most precious thing in existence," declares Xuanzang.

entourage, > companions; **vale of Kashmir,** mountainous region in northern India; **Gangetic plain,** plain of the Ganga River in India

brigands, bandits >

For more on the Silk Road, see Frances Wood's *The Silk Road: Two Thousand Years in the Heart of Asia* (University of California Press, 2002) and *Along the Silk Road,* edited by Elizabeth Ten Grotenhuis (Arthur M. Sackler Gallery, Smithsonian Institution, 2002).

Susan Whitfield is the head of the British Library's Dunhuang Project, which is putting many Silk Road manuscripts on the Internet. Her book *Life along the Silk Road* (University of California Press, 1999) tells the story of the trade route through the lives of a variety of individuals in the late 10th century, including a merchant, a soldier, and a monk. *The Silk Road: Trade, Travel, War, and Faith,* edited by Susan Whitfield (Serindia, 2004), is the catalog of an exhibition held at the British Library; it includes a number of scholarly essays.

For information on the Tang Dynasty, see *Through the Vermilion Gates: A Journey into China's Past,* by Eleanor C. Munro (Pantheon, 1971), and Charles D. Benn's *China's Golden Age: Everyday Life in the Tang Dynasty* (Oxford University Press, 2004).

24. Down and Out

" DU FU, "AT THE CORNER OF THE WORLD," EIGHTH CENTURY

*Du Fu is thought to be the greatest of Chinese poets—he is often
called a god of poetry. His life was not very divine, however. Even
though he came from a family of scholars, he did not pass the difficult
exams that would let him become an important government official.
Instead, as the Tang government he loved was falling apart in the
eighth century because of invaders and war, Du Fu lived as a poor
wanderer. He wrote sad poetry about his career failures and lamented
the warfare and destruction around him. Like other great Chinese
poets, he told his story by using images from nature. These images
help us to discover his feelings at being away from the center of power.*

See chapter 2 of
The Asian World

> By **Yangzi and Han** the mountains pile their barriers.
> A cloud in the wind, at the corner of the world.
> Year in, year out, there's no familiar thing,
> And stop after stop is the end of my road.
> In ruin and discord, the **Prince of Qinchuan**
> Pining in exile, the courtier of **Chu.**
> My heart in peaceful times had cracked already,
> And I walk a road each day more desolate.

< Yangzi and Han, major
Chinese rivers

< Prince of Qinchuan,
an ancient Chinese
ruler; Chu, a powerful
ancient Chinese state

The poems of Du Fu (also spelled Tu Fu) are available in *The
Selected Poems of Tu Fu*, translated by David Hinton (New Directions,
1989). *Three Chinese Poets: Translations of Poems by Wang Wei, Li Bai, and
Du Fu*, translated by Vikram Seth (HarperPerennial, 1993), presents the
works of three Tang dynasty poets. Another collection of Tang poetry, with
poems by Li Bai (also known as Li Po) and Du Fu, is *Bright Moon, Perching
Bird*, translated by J. P. Seaton and James Cryer (Wesleyan University Press,
1987). *Li Po and Tu Fu* is a selection of poems translated and annotated by
Arthur D. Cooper (Penguin, 1973). *Tu Fu*, by A. R. Davis (Twayne, 1971),
is an accessible biography of the poet.

25. Miss Manners

❝ MISS ZHENG, BOOK OF FILIAL PIETY FOR WOMEN, ABOUT 730

See chapters 1 and 2
of *The Asian World*

In the early modern period, Chinese women, like Chinese men, wanted to know how to behave well because they believed in the ideas of the philosopher Confucius, who lived more than a thousand years before. Confucius thought each person's conduct was central to the proper ordering of society. His rules for this conduct involved the "five relations"— between ruler and subject, parent and child, husband and wife, older brother and younger brother, and friend and friend. These relationships were to be based on proper manners and ritually correct behavior, and everyone—even the king—was to show the right kind of consideration for others. The idea was that showing respect and concern could make entire families and kingdoms run well.

Many advice books to guide people in these relationships were written for men, but few addressed the behavior of women. This guidebook to woman's filial piety (duty to parents and husband), which a woman known as Miss Zheng wrote for her niece, became popular. Like the works of Confucius, this guide for women appears as a conversation, in this case between the wise Lady Ban and a group of women questioning her about how to be good. Miss Zheng explains how women from different social groups—from noble ladies to common people—can show "filial piety," and how a woman's behavior relates to the "three powers," the laws of religion, nature, and society.

Lady Ban said . . . "Filial piety expands heaven and earth, deepens human relationships, stimulates the ghosts and spirits, and moves the birds and beasts. It involves being respectful and conforming to ritual, acting only after repeated thought, making no effort to broadcast one's accomplishments or good deeds, being agreeable, gentle, pure, obedient, kind, intelligent, filial, and compassionate. When such virtuous conduct is perfected, no one will reproach you." . . .

The Noble Ladies

"Although occupying honored positions, they are able to show restraint and they can hold their positions without relying on **partiality**.

partiality, favoritism >

They observe the **diligent toil** [of others] and understand their view-points. . . . By first ensuring that their persons conform to **propriety** whether at rest or in motion, they are able to get along well with their children and grandchildren and preserve the ancestral temples. This is the filial piety of the noble ladies. . . ."

< diligent toil, hard work; **propriety**, proper behavior*

The Common People

"They follow the way of the wife and utilize moral principle to the best advantage. They put others first and themselves last in order to serve their parents-in-law. They spin and weave and sew clothes; they prepare the sacrificial foods. This is the filial piety of the wife of a common person." . . .

The Three Powers

The women said, "How exceedingly great is the husband!"

Lady Ban responded, "The husband is heaven. Can one not be devoted to him? In antiquity when a woman went to be married, she was said to be going home. She transfers her heaven to serve her husband. The principle in this is vast. It is the pattern of heaven, the standard of the earth, the **norm** of conduct for the people. When women follow the nature of heaven and earth, model themselves on the brilliance of heaven, make use of the resources of the earth, guard against idleness, and **adhere** to ritual, then they can bring success to their families. On this basis, a wife acts first to extend her love broadly, then her husband will not forget to be filial to his parents. She sets an example of **rectitude** and virtue, and her husband enthusiastically copies it. She takes the initiative in being reverent and yielding, and her husband is not competitive. If she follows the path of ritual and music, her husband will join in harmoniously. If she indicates the difference between good and evil, her husband will know restraint."

< norm, standard*

< adhere, stick*

< rectitude, moral correctness*

For an introduction to Confucianism, see *Confucianism,* by Thomas Hoobler (Facts on File, 1993); *An Introduction to Confucianism,* by Xinzhong Yao (Cambridge University Press, 2000); *Confucianism: A Short Introduction,* by John H. Berthrong (Oneworld, 2000); and *Confucianism: Origins, Beliefs, Practices, Holy Texts, Sacred Places,* by Jennifer Oldstone-

Moore (Oxford University Press, 2002). *Confucius: The Golden Rule*, by Russell Freedman (Arthur A. Levine Books, 2002), is a well-regarded biography of the sage.

26. Love Those Soap Operas

" MURASAKI SHIKIBU, THE TALE OF GENJI, ABOUT 1000

See chapter 5 of *The Asian World*

The Tale of Genji is the story of a brilliant Japanese prince, Genji. Its author, Lady Murasaki, lived in the medieval court in Kyoto in the late 10th century and knew all the gossip, customs, and pastimes of the wealthy, royal, and famous people of her day. She was a member of the powerful Fujiwara family. As a writer, Lady Murasaki brought about a real change in what people read when she made her novel about the adventures and romances of dashing Prince Genji. It is considered one of the first novels ever written in any language. Until her time, Japanese scholars wanted mainly to read Chinese poetry and philosophy, but Murasaki began a trend toward using Japanese in literary writing. In this passage Genji talks about his friend's strange obsession with the fate of characters who—like soap opera heroes of the present day—were not even real. Genji himself is still so popular in Japan that he appears as a hero in cartoons, and there is a rock band called "Shining Prince," another name for Genji.

Tamakasura, a lady > of the court

purveyors, > suppliers

indispensable, > essential

One day Genji, going the round with a number of romances which he had promised to lend, came to **Tamakasura's** room and found her, as usual, hardly able to lift her eyes from the book in front of her. "Really, you are incurable," he said, laughing. "I sometimes think that young ladies exist for no other purpose than to provide **purveyors** of the absurd and improbable with a market for their wares. I am sure that the book you are now so intent upon is full of the wildest nonsense. Yet knowing this all the time, you are completely captivated by its extravagances and follow them with the utmost excitement: why, here you are on this hot day, so hard at work that, though I am sure you have not the least idea of it, your hair is in the most extraordinary tangle. . . . But there; I know quite well that these old tales are **indispensable** during such weather as this. How else would you all manage to get through the day? Now for a confession. I too have lately been studying these books and have, I must tell you, been amazed by the delight which they have given me. There is, it seems, an art of so fitting each part of the narrative into the next that, though all is mere invention, the reader is persuaded that such things might easily have happened and is as deeply moved as though they were actually going on around him. We may know with one part of our minds that every incident has been invented for the express purpose of impressing us; but (if the plot is constructed with the **requisite** skill) we may all the while in another part of our minds be burning with indignation at the wrongs endured by some wholly imaginary princess.

< requisite, necessary

This selection from *The Tale of Genji* is from the classic translation by Arthur Whaley (Modern Library, 1960; Dover, 2000). Another classic translation is by Edward G. Seidensticker (Vintage, 1990). A newer one is by Royall Tyler (Viking, 2001). *The Tale of Genji: Legends and Paintings* (George Braziller, 2001) is a collection of 17th-century images, each of which illustrates one chapter of the novel.

27. Whistle While You Work

RATANBAI, SONG, BETWEEN 12TH AND 14TH CENTURIES

Ordinary people often disappear from history without a trace. This almost happened to Ratanbai, a poet from South Asia. Scholars believe that she was well known in her lifetime, but we have learned little about her except that she lived between the 12th and 14th centuries, and that she was a "bhakti" poet. Bhaktis usually came from the lower classes of artisans and traders, and they believed in intense private worship that was not directed by priests. Their kind of faith opposed the well-educated upper class's control of religion. Instead, bhakti poets wrote about their feelings and experiences and rejected the use of Sanskrit, the "classical" language of scholars, religious leaders, and the nobles of the court. Ratanbai used Gujarati, a language from the west of India, to write this poem about her everyday life of hard work in the household.

See chapter 8
of *The Asian World*

My spinning wheel is dear to me, my sister;
My household depends on it.
My husband married me and departed;
He went abroad to earn a living.

After twelve years he returned,
With a copper coin and a half;
He went to bathe in the **Ganga**,
Dropped the copper coin and a half.

Mother, father, father-in-law, mother-in-law,
One and all rejected us;
The spinning wheel was our savior,
To it we clung.

I paid off all my husband's debts
And over and above
Tying coin after coin in the corner of my **sari**
I earned a whole rupee.

Ganga, also called >
the Ganges, a holy
river in India where
Hindus bathe for
spiritual cleansing

sari, a length of fabric >
draped around the
body, worn by Indian
women

This song comes from an anthology called *Women Writing in India 600 BC to the Present*, edited by Susie Tharu and K. Lalita (Feminist Press, 1991–93). Other sources for Tamil (a language spoken in the southeast Indian state of Tamil Nadu) poetry include Norman Cutler's *Songs of Experience: The Poetics of Tamil Devotion* (Indiana University Press, 1987) and *The Oxford India Ramanujan*, edited by Molly Daniels-Ramanujan (Oxford University Press, 2004).

28. How to Shop and Not Drop

FRANCESCO DI BALDUCCI PEGOLOTTI, GUIDE FOR MERCHANTS, 14TH CENTURY

See chapter 10 of
The European World
and chapter 4 of
The Asian World

In the Middle Ages, goods from Asia slowly made their way into European society, boosting people's appetites for spices to make food taste better, colorful dishes for presenting the food, and luxurious silks that were more beautiful and comfortable than any fabrics Europeans knew how to produce. The Italians, living on the Mediterranean close to trade routes, picked up on this fabulous opportunity to get money and became busy traders. Just as there were advice books for housewives, there were advice books for traders, because setting out on such a long journey across unknown territory could be perilous, and the ways of the Asians were very different from those of the Europeans. Francesco di Balducci Pegolotti, a trader from Florence, Italy, wrote this guide for merchants in the early 14th century, describing the important cities and roads on the way to Asia.

First [of all], from **Tana** to **Astrakhan** it is twenty-five days by ox wagon, and from ten to twelve days by horse wagon. Along the road you meet many Mongolians, that is, armed men. [He gives the number of days for each stretch of the trip thereafter, depending on whether the traveler takes a water or land route, uses camels, donkeys, or horses.]

< **Tana**, believed to be a city in either northern Germany or on the northeastern shore of the Black Sea; **Astrakhan**, city on the Volga River in southern Russia

Things Necessary for a Merchant Wishing to Make the Said Journey to **Cathay**: First [of all], it is advisable for him to let his beard grow long and not shave. And at Tana he should furnish himself with **dragomans**, and he should not try to save by hiring a poor one instead of a good one, since a good one does not cost. . . . And besides dragomans he ought to take along at least two good menservants who know the **Cumanic** tongue well. And if the merchant wishes to take along from Tana any woman with him, he may do so—and if he does not wish to take one, there is no obligation; yet if he takes one, he will be regarded as a man of higher condition than if he does not take one. If he takes one, however, she ought to know the Cumanic tongue as well as the manservant. . . . Wherever you go in the said journey . . . you ought to furnish yourself with flour and salt fish, for other things you find in sufficiency, and especially meat.

< **Cathay**, a European term for China

< **dragomans**, interpreters or guides, especially in countries speaking Arabic, Turkish, or Persian; **Cumanic**, a Turkic language

The road leading from Tana to Cathay is quite safe both by day and by night, according to what the merchants report who have used it—except that if the merchant should die along the road, when going or returning, everything would go to the lord of the country where the merchant dies . . . and in like manner if he should die in Cathay. Actually if he had a brother or a close associate who could say that he is a brother, the property of the dead man would be given to him, and in this manner the property would be rescued. . . .

Cathay is a province where there are many towns and many villages. Among others there is one which is the master city, where merchants **convene** and where is the bulk of trade. . . . And the bulk of said city has a **circuit** of one hundred miles and is all full of people and houses and of dwellers in the said city.

< **convene**, gather
< **circuit**, a circular line around an area

Two good sources about trade along the Silk Road between Europe and China are *Silk Road Encounters: Sourcebook,* by John S. Major (The Silk Road Project and the Asia Society, 2001), and *The Silk Route: 7,000 Miles of History,* by John S. Major and Stephen Fiesser (Harper Trophy, 1996). An overview for younger readers is *Life during the Middle Ages,* by Earle Rice (Lucent, 1998). See also Barbara A. Hanawalt, *The Middle Ages: An Illustrated History* (Oxford University Press, 1998). A good reference is *Trade, Travel, and Exploration in the Middle Ages: An Encyclopedia,* edited by John Block Friedman and Kristen Mossler Figg (Garland, 2000).

29. The Tea Pickers

GAO QI, "THE TEA PICKERS," MID-14TH CENTURY

See chapter 9 of
The Asian World

By the 14th century, the custom of drinking tea had become an important part of life in China, making tea a major crop to sell on the market. The women who picked the tea did not have to follow the normal rules for women's behavior. Unlike most Chinese women, who were expected to lead serious and secluded lives in the "inner quarters" of the household, women tea pickers worked outside and, as one poet portrayed them, were lighthearted, painting their eyebrows and wearing flowers. In this verse by the celebrated poet Gao Qi, they do not get to taste the tea because they must surrender it to high officials and to merchants. The poet is sending many messages at once, protesting what he sees as injustice while describing the tea pickers' lives in romantic terms.

> The rain has passed over creeks and mountains, and the blue clouds are mild;
> In the thick shadows tea leaves are half-sprouted, and shoots are still short.
> The girls in silver hairpins sing back and forth; Looking at each other's baskets, they inquire: "Who has picked the most?"
> The fragrance of the tea leaves is still on their hands when they return;
> The highest grade tea will be first presented to the governor.
> Just cured in the **bamboo brazier**, the tea is so fresh—but they do not taste it;

bamboo brazier, a container for hot coals made of bamboo used to dry the tea leaves >

Packed into baskets, it will be sold to the **Hunan**
　　merchants. The mountain people do not know about
　　growing rice and **millet**;
Year after year they rely on the tea harvest season for their
　　sustenance.

< **Hunan,** province of
　southeastern China

< **millet,** a type of grain

< **sustenance,** means of
　support

📖　This selection comes from the collection *Under Confucian Eyes:
Writings on Gender in Chinese History,* by Susan Mann and Yu-Yin Cheng
(University of California Press, 2001). *Women Writers of Traditional China:
An Anthology of Poetry and Criticism,* edited by Kang-i San Chang and
Haun Saussy (Stanford University Press, 1999), is another interesting col-
lection of poetry by Chinese women. For the history of women in China,
see Patricia Buckley Ebrey's *Women and the Family in Chinese History*
(Routledge, 2003).

On the history of the tea industry, see *The Empire of Tea: The
Remarkable History of the Plant that Took Over the World,* by Alan Macfarlane
(Overlook, 2004). *Tea: Addiction, Exploitation, and Empire,* by Roy Moxham
(Carroll & Graf, 2003), explains how tea was imported to England. *Chinese
Tea Culture,* by Ling Wang (Foreign Language Press, 2000), describes the
role of tea in traditional Chinese culture, and *Steeped in Tea: Creative Ideas,
Activities & Recipes for Tea Lovers,* by Diana Rosen (Storey Books, 1999),
has a chapter on "Traditional Eastern Tea Events." *A Time for Tea: Travels
through China and India in Search of Tea,* by Jason Goodwin (Knopf, 1991),
is a travel writer's account of the modern tea trade.

30. Water, Water Everywhere

❝ KING MUNJONG, EDICT, 1451

*Korea prospered in the 15th century as it improved its agriculture
and in particular started planting rice in wet land, rather than in dry
soil. This made well-organized projects for irrigating farmland very
important. Two forward-looking Korean monarchs—King Sejong, who
ruled from 1418 to 1450, and his son Munjong, who died in 1452 at
the age of 38—sponsored many improvements to farming. Despite his
youth, Munjong had real vision when it came to agriculture and irrigation. Following the lead of his father, who had ordered the writing
of a helpful guide called* Straight Talk on Farming, *Munjong issued
this edict, or official order, on irrigation to the governors of various
Korean states in 1451.*

See chapter 11 of
The Asian World

water mills, places>
for grinding grain
powered by water run-
ning over a wheel;
misfortunes,
crop failures

As I considered the intent of former kings in the construction of **water mills,** and as I contemplated day and night the ways to save those people in the northern provinces who have been the victims of this year's **misfortunes,** I came to the conclusion that nothing is more urgent than the work on river embankments and other irrigation. Some may insist that no advantages will come from the construction of new irrigation works. I, however, disagree with this thinking. If we accept the notion that all that can be done has been done by men in the past and that hence there is no room for new considerations, how can there be cotton in our country, which was introduced not long ago, and how can we have the benefit of refined gunpowder, which was not developed until the year [1445]. There have been many other similar developments in recent years. If we had followed these people, we would not be enjoying the benefit of these things.

reclamation of>
wetland, making
swamp or marshland
useful for agriculture

When I consulted with the ministers, they all said there is no need to send officials [to oversee the improvements]; instead they counseled that I should issue a royal edict to the governors of these provinces urging them to promote the **reclamation of wetland.** You, governors, knowing this situation, should make the villagers understand my intention and guide them in realizing the advantages of wetland. Then there will be some who recognize the advantages of wetland. Then there will be some who recognize the advantages and will in turn lead other people so that they too may respond favorably. After meeting and discussing this with the people, you should reclaim as much wetland as possible, either by means of spring water

embankments,>
raised structures of
earth used to hold
back water; feasible,
possible

or by constructing river **embankments.** After carefully investigating whether or not the works are **feasible** and whether or not the people favor them, you should submit a report to me.

This document is one of many in the very important anthology *Sources of Korean Tradition: From Early Times through the Sixteenth Century,* edited by Peter H. Lee and William Theodore deBary (Columbia University Press, 1997–2000). A good general history is *Korea: An Illustrated History, from Ancient Times to 1945,* by David Rees (Hippocrene, 2001).

The Art of Rice: Spirit and Sustenance in Asia, by Roy W. Hamilton (UCLA Fowler Museum of Cultural History, 2003), is a beautifully illustrated book that describes the role of rice in Asian cultures. *Rice*, by Sylvia A. Johnson (Lerner, 1985), is a short book on how rice is grown as a food crop around the world. *The Story of Rice*, by Leonard S. Kenworthy (Julian Messner, 1979), is a similar book that describes the growing and uses of rice. Peter Chrisp's *The Farmer through History* (Thomson Learning, 1993) is a broader view of farming for young readers.

31. Oh, Give Me a Child

ANONYMOUS FOLK SONG, DATE UNKNOWN

Women in early modern South Asia, though unable to read or write, still composed poetry and songs. They often recited these poems while working or sang them as a group while doing chores together. These poems generally talk of everyday tasks and household affairs. They sometimes call out to Krishna, an important South Asian god, and other spirits, asking them to grant their wishes. Because they were not written down until much later but rather recited like nursery rhymes or sung like lullabies, we do not know the exact date when they were composed. The singer here is sad because her husband's family blames her for not having had a baby, even though she works hard for the household. Because children, especially as they grew up, were expected to work and help their families, having babies was a woman's most important job.

See chapters 3, 4, and 8 of *The Asian World*

> My courtyard has been cleaned and plastered
> Give me a child who will print it with his footsteps,
>> O **Rannade**
> Mother, the taunts of childlessness are hard to bear.
>
> I stand here after grinding the grain,
> Give me a child who will scatter the heap of flour, O
>> Rannade!
> Mother, the taunts of childlessness are hard to bear.
>
> I stand here after fetching water from the river,
> Give me a child who will hang on to the corner of my sari,
>> O Rannade!
> Mother, the taunts of childlessness are hard to bear.

< A statue of **Rannade**, the sun queen, is placed in the house of a woman who is expecting her first child

curds, lumps of >
curdled milk that can
be made into cheese
or butter

I stand here after churning the **curds,**
Give me a child who will demand butter, O Rannade!
Mother, the taunts of childlessness are hard to bear.

chapati, thin, >
flat bread similar
to a tortilla

I stand here after cooking the **chapatis,**
Give me a child who will ask for a tiny one, O Rannade!
Mother, the taunts of childlessness are hard to bear.

I am wearing a clean white sari,
Give me a child who will spring up and down in my lap,
    O Rannade!
Mother, the taunts of childlessness are hard to bear.

A useful general anthology of Asian literature is *Great Literature of the Eastern World: The Major Works of Prose, Poetry, and Drama from China, India, Japan, Korea, and the Middle East,* edited by Ian P. McGreal (HarperCollins, 1996). *Shower of Gold: Girls and Women in the Stories of India,* by Uma Krishnaswami (Linnet, 1999), is an annotated collection of stories featuring strong female figures from Hindu mythology, Buddhist tales, and the history and folklore of the Indian subcontinent.

AN AGE OF EMPIRES, 1200–1750

32. The End of the World

**'ALA-AD-DIN 'ATA-MALIK JUVAINI, THE HISTORY OF
THE WORLD CONQUEROR, 13TH CENTURY**

*The Mongol conquest of much of Asia and parts of Europe was an
unforgettable moment in human history. The Mongols—tribes of
nomads from Central Asia—devastated the peoples who stood in their
path, but they also ended up encouraging the exchange of ideas, the
spread of religions, and the expansion of trade among the societies
they conquered. Before they could recognize those benefits, however,
most people thought they were seeing the end of the world, so cruel
were the Mongol invaders. After they had conquered a region, the
Mongols used talented local people to govern for them.*

See chapters 1 and
2 of *An Age of
Empires*, chapter 7
of *The Asian World*,
and chapter 1 of
An Age of Voyages

*A Muslim who came from a long line of government officials,
'Ala-ad-Din 'Ata-Malik Juvaini, the author of this account of the
Mongol invasion, worked for the Mongols after they invaded and
came to admire their toleration in matters of religion. He even wrote
their history, but he did not shy away from describing how the
invaders mercilessly slaughtered his people. Juvaini tells about the
brutal tactics of the Mongols, who had already killed about 70,000
Turkish nomads outside the wealthy city of Merv (in present-day
Turkmenistan) when, in 1221, they forced the town to surrender.*

[The Mongol leader] Toli questioned [the governor of Merv] about
the town and asked for details regarding the wealthy and notable.
Mujir-al-Mulk [the governor] gave him a list of two hundred persons, and Toli ordered them to be brought into his presence. Of the

"the Earth quaked > with her quaking," from the Quran, expresses the people's fear; "the Earth cast forth her burdens," also from the Quran, explains that the invaders took the people's treasure from the ground.

peri-like, resembling > beautiful supernatural beings; artisans, craftspeople

levies, recruits >

citadel, fortress; > maqsura, a stall in the mosque reserved for the religious leader, or imam

cavities, hollowed- > out spaces

rearguard, soldiers > who protect the back of the main army

cast into well of > annihilation, threw into the well of death, or killed; Nishapur, city in northeastern Iran

sayyid, title given > to noble Muslims descended from founders of the Shi'ite branch of Islam; piety, devoutness, devotion to religion

questioning of these persons one might have said that "**the Earth quaked with her quaking**" and of the digging up of their buried possessions, both money and goods, that "**the Earth cast forth her burdens**."

The Mongols now entered the town and drove all the inhabitants, nobles and commoners, out onto the plain. For four days and nights the people continued to come out of the town; the Mongols detained them all, separating the women from the men. Alas! How many **peri-like** ones did they drag from the bosoms of their husbands! How many sisters did they separate from their brothers!

The Mongols ordered that, apart from four hundred **artisans** whom they specified and selected from amongst the men and some children, girls and boys, whom they bore off into captivity, the whole population, including the women and children, should be killed, and no one, whether woman or man, be spared. The people of Merv were then distributed among the soldiers and **levies**, and, in short, to each man was allotted the execution of three or four hundred persons.

Then, at Toli's command, the outworks were destroyed, the **citadel** leveled with the ground and the *maqsura* of the mosque belonging to the sect of the greatest *imam* Abu-Hanifa (*God have mercy on him!*) set on fire.

When the army departed, those that had sought refuge in holes and **cavities** came out again, and there were gathered together some five thousand persons. A party of Mongols belonging to the **rearguard** then arrived and wished to have their share of slaughter. They commanded therefore that each person should bring a skirtful of grain out onto the plain for the Mongols; and in this way they **cast into the well of annihilation** most of those that had previously escaped. Then they proceeded along the road to **Nishapur** and slew all they found of those who had turned back from the plain and fled from the Mongols when halfway out to meet them.

Now the *sayyid* 'Izz-ad-Din Nassaba was one of the great *sayyids* and renowned for his **piety** and virtue. He now together with other persons passed thirteen days and nights in counting the people slain within the town. Taking into account only those that were plain to see and leaving aside those that had been killed in holes and cavities and in the villages and deserts, they arrived at a figure of more than one million three hundred thousand.

Javaini's *Genghis Khan: The History of the World Conqueror,* in the standard translation by J. A. Boyle, has been published with a new bibliography by David O. Morgan (University of Washington Press, 1997). Morgan is also the author of the survey *The Mongols* (Blackwell, 1990). *The Devil's Horsemen: The Mongol Invasion of Europe,* by James Chambers (Atheneum, 1979), covers military and diplomatic affairs, while *The Mongols,* by Stephen R. Turnbull (Osprey, 1986), is an illustrated guide to Mongol military operations. *The Mongol Conquests: Time Frame AD 1200–1300* (Time-Life Books, 1989) is an illustrated history of the Mongol Empire. *Genghis Khan and the Making of the Modern World,* by anthropologist Jack Weatherford (Crown, 2004), describes the Mongol military campaigns and gives a new interpretation of Genghis Khan's personality. *Conquerors on Horseback,* by Daniel Cohen (Doubleday, 1970), and *The Mongol Empire,* by Mary Hull (Lucent, 1998), are written for young adults.

33. Top Model: Isabella, Queen of Spain

ANONYMOUS MANUSCRIPT, BETWEEN 1469 AND 1474

Isabella of Castile, queen of Spain from 1474 to1504, was a powerful, intelligent, and devout ruler. Her religious faith led her to try to rid Spain of Islamic influence and to persecute Jews and other non-Christians. She was shrewd in supporting the travels of Christopher Columbus, which eventually allowed Spain to become far richer than it was before. Yet some supporters, such as the anonymous author of this unpublished manuscript, described her in a totally different way by talking about her personal qualities. This passage describes the young Isabella before she became queen. We wonder why this person close to Isabella's court chose not to sign this highly favorable account, which was written some time between the late 1460s and the mid-1470s.

See chapter 9 of *An Age of Empires* and chapter 10 of *An Age of Voyages*

The Princess had blue-green eyes with long eyelashes, full of sparkle along with great frankness and dignity. High arching eyebrows much enhanced the beauty of her eyes and **countenance.** Her nose was of   <countenance, face
a size and shape that made her face more beautiful. Her mouth was small and red, her teeth small and white. Her laughter was quiet and

controlled; rarely was she seen to laugh in the customary manner of youth, but with restraint and moderation. In this and in all things the character and honor of womanly virtue shone in her face. She was regarded with such respect that no great prince who dealt with *audacity, boldness >* her had the **audacity** to be in the least discourteous to her. From her childhood she was brought up by her mother in honesty and virginal purity, so that never did her worst enemy find any reason or suggestion to stain her reputation. Her face colored readily under its white *mien, expression >* skin, and was of royal **mien**. Her hair was very long and golden-red, and she would often run her hands through it, to arrange it so as bet- *configuration, >* ter to display the **configuration** of her face. Her throat was high, full *arrangement* and rounded, as women prefer it to be; her hands were exquisitely graceful; all her body and her person were as lovely as a woman's could be. She was moderately tall. In person and countenance no one in her time touched her perfection, refinement, and purity. Her *aspect, appearance >* **aspect** as she moved, and the beauty of her face, were luminous.

There are many biographies of Queen Isabella. Two for young adults are *First Lady of the Renaissance: A Biography of Isabella d'Este*, by Edith Patterson Meyer (Little, Brown, 1970), and *Ferdinand and Isabella*, by Paul Stevens (Chelsea House, 1988). There are also quite a few full-length biographies: *Ferdinand and Isabella*, by Felipe Fernández-Armesto, (Taplinger, 1975); *The Bed and the Throne: The Life of Isabella d'Este*, by George Marek (Harper & Row, 1976); *Isabel the Queen: Life and Times*, by Peggy K. Liss (Oxford University Press, 1992); and *Isabella of Castile: The First Renaissance Queen*, by Nancy Rubin (St. Martin's, 1991).

34. Wish You Were Here

66 CHRISTOPHER COLUMBUS, LETTER TO QUEEN ISABELLA, 1492

See chapter 9 of *An Age of Empires* and chapter 10 of *An Age of Voyages*

In 1492, Christopher Columbus, sponsored by the monarchs Ferdinand and Isaballa of Spain, entered what he called the "Indian Sea," really the Caribbean, and found many islands, which he claimed on behalf of his royal patrons. He then went to what he called Hispana, the island Hispaniola—now divided between the countries of Haiti and the Dominican Republic. There, he found not only plenty of riches but also remarkable people about whom he had mixed feelings.

He felt that the islanders had real affection for the Europeans and sent this observation back to the queen in this letter, which was later published as a pamphlet. Such writing was a kind of publicity to the world about Spanish achievements in exploration.

In . . . Hispana, there are very lofty and beautiful mountains, great farms, groves and fields, most fertile both for **cultivation** and for **pasturage**, and well adapted for constructing buildings. The convenience of the harbors in this island, and the excellence of the rivers, in volume and **salubrity**, surpass human belief, unless one should see them. In it the trees, pasturelands, and fruits differ much from those of **Johana**. Besides, this Hispana abounds in various kinds of spices, gold, and metals. The inhabitants of both sexes of this and of all of the other islands I have seen, or of which I have any knowledge, always go as naked as they came into the world, except that some of the women cover parts of their bodies with leaves or branches, or a veil of cotton, which they prepare themselves for this purpose. They are all, as I said before, unprovided with any sort of iron, and they are **destitute of arms**, which are entirely unknown to them, and for which they are not adapted; not on account of any bodily deformity, for they are well-made, but because they are timid and full of terror. . . . They are very **guileless** and honest, and very **liberal of** all they have. No one refuses the asker anything that he possesses; on the contrary, they themselves invite us to ask for it. They manifest affection toward all of us, exchanging valuable things for **trifles**, content with the very least thing or nothing at all.

They do not practise **idolatry**; on the contrary, they believe that all strength, all power, in short, all blessings, are from Heaven, and that I have come down from there with these ships and sailors; and in this spirit was I received everywhere, after they had got over their fear. They are neither lazy nor awkward, but, on the contrary, are of an excellent and acute understanding. Those who have sailed these seas give excellent accounts of everything; but they have never seen men wearing clothes, or ships like ours.

< **cultivation**, growing crops; **pasturage**, fields for grazing animals

< **salubrity**, health

< **Johana**, present-day Cuba, which Columbus named Johana after the princess of Spain

< **destitute of arms**, completely without weapons

< **guileless**, innocent; **liberal of**, generous with

< **trifles**, things of little or no value; **idolatry**, worship of images of gods

The first biography of Columbus was by his son Ferdinand, published as *The Life of the Admiral Christopher Columbus by His Son*

Ferdinand, translated by Benjamin Keen (Rutgers University Press, 1992). There are numerous biographies for young adults: Zachary Kent's *Christopher Columbus* (Children's Press, 1991); Colin Hynson's *Columbus and the Renaissance Explorers* (Barron's, 2000); *Christopher Columbus and the First Voyages to the New World,* by Steven Dodge (Chelsea House, 1991); and *The Voyages of Columbus,* by Richard Humble (Franklin Watts, 1991).

Columbus's own diaries have been published as *I, Columbus: My Journal, 1492–3,* edited by Peter and Connie Roop (Walker, 1990; Avon, 1990); *First Voyage to America: From the Log of the "Santa Maria"* (1938; reprint, Dover, 1991); and *The Voyage of Christopher Columbus: Columbus's Own Journal of Discovery,* in a new translation by John Cummins (St. Martin's, 1992). His correspondence can be found in *The Authentic Letters of Columbus,* with an introduction by William Eleroy Curtis (Field Columbia Museum, 1895); *Four Voyages to the New World: Letters and Selected Documents,* translated and edited by R. H. Major and introduced by John E. Fagg (Carol Publishing, 1992); and in *Select Letters of Christopher Columbus* (Corinth Books, 1961).

35. Wrecking the Place

HANS MAYR, MEMOIR, 1505

See chapter 8 of
An Age of Empires
and chapter 13
of *The African
and Middle
Eastern World*

Late in the 15th century, Europeans began extensive exploration of the world, and they started to get rich from their voyages. Their wealth came mostly from stealing other people's goods, because the Europeans were fairly far behind Asian and African countries in having valuable things to trade. What they did have were very big guns. In 1505 the Portuguese decided that they would simply shoot their way in and loot, or "sack," the thriving cities of Kilwa and Mombasa on the East African coast. Although many of the Africans' buildings were made of stone, some were not, and the Portuguese burned these to drive out the inhabitants in order to take their goods. This account of what happened is usually attributed to Hans Mayr, a German traveler on one of the eight Portuguese ships, but the identity of the author is not known for certain. Although the sailors who stole the goods did get some of the stolen property, typically most of it went to the king, the captain, and any investors in the voyages.

Grand-Captain,
commander of a fleet
of ships >

The **Grand-Captain** ordered that the town should be sacked and that each man should carry off to his ship whatever he found: so that at the end there would be a division of the **spoil**, each man to receive a twentieth of what he found. The same rule was made for gold, silver, and pearls. Then everyone started to plunder the town and to search the houses, forcing open the doors with axes and iron bars. There was a large quantity of cotton cloth for **Sofala** in the town, for the whole coast gets its cotton cloth from here. So the Grand-Captain got a good share of the trade of Sofala for himself. A large quantity of rich silk and gold embroidered clothes was seized, and carpets also; one of these which was without equal for beauty, was sent to the King of Portugal together with many other valuables.

   . . . On the morning of the 16th they again plundered the town, but because the men were tired from fighting and from lack of sleep, much of the wealth was left behind apart from what each man took for himself. They also carried away provisions, rice, honey, butter, **maize**, countless camels and a large number of cattle, and even two elephants. They paraded these elephants in front of the people of the town before they took it, in order to frighten them. There were many prisoners, and white women among them and children, and also some merchants from **Cambay**.

> <**spoil**, goods taken from an enemy

> <**Sofala**, port city in Mozambique

> <**maize**, corn

> <**Cambay**, port city in India, north of Bombay

   The most recent scholarly book on the Portuguese Empire is *A History of Portuguese Overseas Expansion, 1400–1668,* by Malyn Newitt (Routledge, 2004). Some earlier books on the Portuguese explorers are *Vasco da Gama and his Successors, 1460–1580,* by K. G. Jayne (Barnes & Noble, 1970); *Portuguese Africa,* by Ronald H. Chilcote (Prentice-Hall, 1967); *The History of Portugal,* by James M. Anderson (Greenwood, 2000); and *The Portugal Story: Three Centuries of Exploration and Discovery,* by the novelist John Dos Passos (Doubleday, 1969). *The Explorers,* by Richard Humble and the editors of Time-Life Books (Time-Life Books, 1978), is a beautifully illustrated account of Spanish and Portuguese exploration. On the Portuguese explorers in general, a good book for young adults is *Vasco da Gama and the Portuguese Explorers,* by Rebecca Stefoff (Chelsea House, 1993).

36. Turkish Delight

SULTAN MEHMED II, QUOTED IN AN ANONYMOUS MANUSCRIPT, 1510

See chapter 6 of
An Age of Empires

The Ottoman Turks, a group of Turkic peoples who came from Asia, set up a successful empire in the 14th century and steadily expanded its borders in Asia Minor (present-day Turkey), the Middle East, and North Africa, and eventually into eastern Europe. In 1453 they finally captured the city of Constantinople, the center of the fading Byzantine Empire, and made it their capital. Having defeated the Christians in a series of ongoing struggles, Sultan Mehmed II, known as the Conqueror, boastfully explained the Christians' defeat. His analysis—like many written by triumphant peoples—attributed the losers' defeat to their inferiority and also to the will of God. The idea behind many empires for as long as they survived was that heaven or other powerful forces in the universe were on their side. Religious superiority, the winners thought, explained their victory. This record of the sultan's words comes from a Serbian manuscript written around 1510.

Gyaours, Muslim word for Christians, from Arabic for "nonbeliever" >

You know well the unwashed **Gyaours** and their ways and manners, which certainly are not fine. They are . . . sleepy, easily shocked, inactive; they like to drink much and to eat much; in misfortunes they are impatient, and in times of good fortune proud and overbearing.

repose, rest >

They are lovers of **repose**, and do not like to sleep without soft feather-beds. . . . They are ignorant of any military stratagems. They keep horses only to ride while hunting with their dogs. . . . They are

menial, lowly >

unable to bear hunger, or cold, or heat, effort and **menial** work. . . .

And then, the Christians fight constantly among themselves, because everyone desires to be a king, or a prince, or the first amongst

concord, agreement, harmony >

them. . . . Fear them not; there is no **concord** amongst them. Every one takes care of himself only; no one thinks of the common interest. They are quarrelsome, unruly, self-willed and disobedient. Obedience to their superiors and discipline they have none, and yet everything depends on that.

When they lose a battle, they always say: "We are not well prepared!" or "This or that traitor has betrayed us!" or "We were too few in number and the Turks were far more numerous!" or "The Turks came upon us without previous declaration of war by misleading representations and **treachery**. They have occupied our country by turning our internal difficulties to their own advantage!"

< treachery, trickiness or treason

Well, that is what they say, being not willing to confess truly and rightly: "God is on the side of the Turks! It is God who helps them, and therefore they conquer us."

Constantinople: The Forgotten Empire, by Isaac Asimov (Houghton Mifflin, 1970), traces the history of Constantinople and the Byzantine Empire from the 7th century BCE to the 15th century CE. *A Short History of Byzantium,* by the noted British scholar John Julius Norwich (Knopf, 1997), is an accessible condensation of his magisterial three-volume history. *Byzantium: The Bridge from Antiquity to the Middle Ages,* by Michael Angold (St. Martin's Press, 2001), is a concise analysis of this pivotal civilization. *The Byzantine Empire,* by James A. Corrick (Lucent, 1997), is a good introduction for young adults. *Constantine,* by Nancy Zinsser Walworth (Chelsea House, 1989), is a useful biography.

There are several good histories of the Ottoman Empire: *Lords of the Horizons: A History of the Ottoman Empire,* by Jason Goodwin (Henry Holt, 1999); *The Ottoman Centuries: The Rise and Fall of the Turkish Empire,* by John Patrick Kinross (Morrow, 1977); and *The Ottomans,* by Andrew Wheatcroft (Viking, 1993).

37. It Was Harsh

ANONYMOUS, ANNALS OF TLATELOLCO, 1528–1531

The invasion of Mexico from 1519 to 1521, led by the Spanish conquistador, or conqueror, Hernán Cortés, ultimately overturned the powerful, sophisticated Aztec Empire and devastated its people. In 1521, Cortés decided to conquer the Aztecs once and for all, and his three-month campaign to defeat them was particularly grim. All parts of Aztec society—from government to families—fell apart, and bloodshed prevailed. Aztec writers produced this account of the campaign sometime between 1528 and 1531. It was written as a traditional lament, a song of grief, and set down in the Aztecs' language, Nahua, as part of a larger history of their civilization called the Annals of Tlatelolco, *the records of an Aztec city founded in 1358.*

See chapter 9 of *An Age of Empires* and chapter 12 of *An Age of Voyages*

And all this happened among us. We saw it. We lived
    through it with an astonishment worthy of tears and of
    pity for the pain we suffered.

shaft, the pole of >
a spear

On the roads lie broken **shafts** and torn hair,
houses are roofless, homes are stained red,
worms swarm in the streets, walls are spattered with brains.
The water is reddish, like dyed water;

brine, salt water; >
saltpeter, a salty sub-
stance used in making
gunpowder; **adobe,**
building material made
from dried earth, or
clay, and straw

we drink it so, we even drink **brine;**
the water we drink is full of **saltpeter.**
The wells are crammed with **adobe** bricks.

Whatever was still alive was kept between shields, like
    precious treasure, between shields, until it was eaten.

tzompantli, altar >
where the skulls of
Aztec sacrificial
victims were usually
displayed; *zacatl,* straw

We chewed on hard **tzompantli** wood, brackish **zacatl** fod-
    der, chunks of adobe, lizards, vermin, dust and worms.

We eat what was on the fire, as soon as it is done we eat it
    together right by the fire.

price, the amount
paid for a slave >

We had a single **price**; there was a standard price for a
    youth, a priest, a boy and a young girl. The maximum

tortillas, flat, round
bread made from corn
or wheat >
brackish, slightly >
salty; **mantles,** capes

price for a slave amounted to only two handfuls of
maize, to only ten **tortillas.** Only twenty bundles of
brackish fodder was the price of gold, jade, **mantles** . . .
all valuables fetched the same low price. It went down

battering engine, >
wheeled structure used
to knock down walls

further when the Spaniards set up their **battering engine**
in the marketplace.

Cuauhtemoc, >
king of the Aztecs

Now, **Cuauhtemoc** orders the prisoners to be brought out;
    the guards don't miss any. The elders and chiefs grab

extremities, >
hands and feet

them by their **extremities** and Cuauhtemoc slits open
their bellies with his own hand.

    This excerpt from the *Annals of Tlatelolco* comes from Gordon
Brotherston's *Image of the New World: The American Continent Portrayed in
Native Texts* (Thames and Hudson, 1979). Another native account is *The
Broken Spears: The Aztec Account of the Conquest of Mexico,* edited by
Miguel León-Portilla (Beacon, 1990). There are several histories of Cortés's
conquest of the Aztecs, including Hugh Thomas's *Conquest: Cortes,
Montezuma, and the Fall of Old Mexico* (Simon and Schuster, 1995) and,

for young adults, Patricia Calvert's *Hernando Cortes: Fortune Favored the Bold* (Benchmark, 2002). On the Aztec Empire itself, see *The Aztecs,* by Frances Berdan (Chelsea House, 1989); *Aztecs: Reign of Blood and Splendor* by the editors of Time-Life Books (Time-Life Books, 1992); and *The Aztec Empire,* by Felipe Solis (Solomon R. Guggenheim Foundation, 2004), the catalog of an extensive exhibition at the Guggenheim Museum in New York City.

38. Taking over Korea—and China— or Maybe Neither

" **REPORT TO HIDEYOSHI, 1592**

Toyotomi Hideyoshi was a poor boy who became the ruler of Japan. The ambition that helped him struggle to the top also made him want to control a vast empire in Asia—much as other Asian leaders had done before him. China and Korea were his specific targets, and his ministers wrote this plan for invading China while Hideyoshi's armies were already on the move to Korea. A military force estimated in the hundreds of thousands reached the Korean capital of Seoul, but when Hideyoshi suddenly died in 1598, the Japanese campaign collapsed. Unlike those of the Mongol leader Khubilai Khan, Russia's Ivan the Terrible, and Spain's Ferdinand and Isabella, Hideyoshi's plans for empire did not work out.

> See introduction and chapters 1 and 9 of *An Age of Empires* and chapter 11 of *The Asian World*

[1] Your Lordship must not relax preparations for the campaign. The departure must by made by the First or Second Month of the coming year.

[2] The Capital of Korea fell on the second day of this month. Thus, the time has come to make the sea crossing and to bring the length and breadth of the **Great Ming** under our control. My desire is that Your Lordship make the crossing to become the **Civil Dictator** of Great China.

< **Great Ming**, territory of the Ming dynasty, which ruled China from 1368 to 1644

< **Civil Dictator**, ruler just below the emperor

[3] Thirty thousand men should accompany you. The departure should be by boat from **Hyogo**. Horses should be sent by land.

< **Hyogo**, city in Japan, now called Kobe

[4] Although no hostility is expected in the Three Kingdoms [Korea], armed preparedness is of the utmost importance, not

only for the maintenance of our reputation but also in the event of an emergency. All subordinates shall be so instructed. . . .

[Items 5 through 17 deal with supplying, equipping, and staffing the expeditionary force.]

[18] Since His Majesty is to be transferred to the Chinese capital, due preparation is necessary. The **imperial visit** will take place the year after next. On that occasion, ten provinces adjacent to the **Capital** shall be **presented** to him. In time instruction will be issued for the **enfeoffment** of all courtiers. Subordinates will receive ten times as much [as their present holdings]. The enfeoffment of those in the upper ranks shall be according to personal qualifications.

imperial visit, official visit by the emperor >

Capital, Beijing; > **presented**, formally awarded as part of his triumph in China; **enfeoffment**, grants of land and other holdings to subordinates

[19] The post of Civil Dictator of China shall be assigned, as aforementioned, to **Hidetsugu** who will be given 100 provinces adjacent to the Capital. The post of Civil Dictator of Japan will go to either the **Middle Counsellor Yamato**, or to the **Bizen Minister**, upon declaration by either of his readiness. . . .

Hidetsugu, > Hideyoshi's adopted son, who ruled after his death; **Middle Counsellor Yamato**, Hideyoshi's half-brother Hidenaga; **Bizen Minister**, his adopted son (yushi) Ukita Hideie

[23] Korea and China are within easy reach, and no inconvenience is anticipated for any concerned, high or low. It is not expected that anyone in those countries will attempt to flee. Therefore, recall all commissioners in the provinces to assist in preparation for the expedition.

This document comes from the standard anthology *Sources of the Japanese Tradition*, edited by Ryusaku Tsunoda, William Theodore deBary, and Donald Keene (Columbia University Press, 1958; a second edition was issued in 2001). *Giants of Japan: The Lives of Japan's Greatest Men and Women*, by Mark Weston (Kodansha International, 1999), includes a chapter entitled "Toyotomi Hideyoshi: The Peasant Who United All of Japan." The only full biography is *Hideyoshi*, by Mary Elizabeth Berry, part of the Harvard East Asian Monographs series (Harvard University Press, 1989).

On Japanese military affairs, see *Life among the Samurai*, by Eleanor J. Hall (Lucent, 1999); *The Book of the Samurai: The Warrior Class of Japan*, by Stephen R. Turnbull (PRC, 2001). There are several good one-volume histories of Japan: *The Japanese Experience: A Short History of Japan*, by W.

G. Beasley (University of California Press, 1999); the classic *Japan, Tradition, and Transformation,* by Edwin O. Reischauer (Houghton Mifflin, 1989); and the more specialized *A History of Japan, 1582–1941: Internal and External Worlds,* by L. M. Cullen (Cambridge University Press, 2003).

39 Live and Let Live

" **'ABD UL-QADIR BADA'UNI, HISTORY OF MUSLIM INDIA, ABOUT 1590**

Conquerors from Central Asia called Mughals set up an empire in India in the 1520s. They brought with them their Islamic faith, but they did not try to change local customs and beliefs. One Mughal leader became renowned for his toleration of other people's religions. His name was Akbar, and he ruled the Mughal Empire in the 16th century. At first Akbar enforced Islamic law, but he soon began to study various religions and listen to leaders from many different religions debate their beliefs. He even stopped eating meat from time to time, the way some Hindus and Buddhists did. In the 18th century, European thinkers who wanted Catholics and Protestants to stop fighting and killing each other over religion pointed to Akbar's tolerant policies as models to be followed in their own countries.

> See chapter 5 of
> *An Age of Empires,*
> chapter 6 of
> *An Age of Voyages,*
> and chapter 4 of
> *An Age of Science
> and Revolutions*

The historian 'Abd ul-Qadir Bada'uni wrote this account of Akbar's interest in different religions, even though he personally opposed Akbar's policy of religious toleration and believed that he was out to destroy Islam altogether. In this passage, Bada'uni describes some of the many religions that Akbar studied, hiding his full feelings about Akbar's openness so that he could keep his job in the government.

[The emperor] used to spend much time in the Hall of Worship in the company of learned men and **sheikhs** and especially on Friday nights, when he would sit up there the whole night continually occupied in discussing questions of religion. . . . The controversies [of different branches of Islam] . . . would attack the very bases of belief. . . . And persons of **novel and whimsical** opinions . . . cast the emperor, who was possessed of an excellent disposition, and was an earnest searcher after truth, but very ignorant and a mere **tyro**, and used to the company of **infidels** and **base persons**, into perplexity, till doubt was heaped upon doubt . . . so that after five or six years not a trace of Islam was left in him; and everything was topsy-turvy. . . .

< **sheikhs,** Muslim religious authorities

novel and whimsical, new and playful, or < unpredictable

< **tyro,** beginner; **infidels,** nonbelievers in a particular religion; **base persons,** immoral people

Samanas, Hindu or >
Buddhist holy persons;
Brahmans, Hindu
priests; fallacy,
falseness

Padre, "father"
in Spanish >

Papa, Italian for >
"father," meaning the
pope; Trinity, the
Father, Son, and Holy
Ghost, that is God,
Jesus, and the Holy
Spirit; doctrines,
teachings; Prince
Murad, Akbar's son;
Abu'l Fah'd probably a
court official

And **Samanas** and **Brahmans** . . . brought forward proofs, based on reason and traditional testimony, for the truth of their own, and the **fallacy** of our religion. . . . And [the Emperor] made his courtiers continually listen to those revilings and attacks against our pure and easy, bright and holy faith [of Islam]. . . .

Learned monks also from Europe, who are called *Padre,* and have an infallible head, called *Papa* . . . brought the Gospel, and advanced proofs for the **Trinity.** His Majesty firmly believed in the truth of the Christian religion, and wishing to spread the **doctrines** of Jesus, ordered **Prince Murad** to take a few lessons in Christianity . . . and charged **Abu'l Fah'd** to translate the Gospel.

This description of Akbar is printed in the standard anthology *Sources of Indian Tradition,* edited by William Theodore deBary (Columbia University Press, 1958); a new edition was issued in 1988. For more on the Mughals, see *India and the Mughal Dynasty,* by Valerie Bérinstain, a beautifully illustrated volume in the Discoveries series (Abrams, 1998), which also contains many primary sources. John F. Richards, *The Mughal Empire,* a volume in the New Cambridge History of India (Cambridge University Press, 1996), and Annemarie Schimmel's *The Empire of the Great Mughals: History, Art, and Culture* (Reaktion Books, 2004) are other good general histories. Useful scholarly works are *Akbar and His India,* by Irfan Habib (Oxford University Press, 1997); *The Formation of the Mughal Empire,* by Douglas E. Streusand (Oxford University Press, 2001); and *Mughal India and Central Asia,* by Richard Foltz (Oxford University Press, 1998).

40. No Rest for the Weary

❝ ALEXANDER RADISHCHEV, A JOURNEY FROM ST. PETERSBURG TO MOSCOW, 1790

See chapter 4 of
An Age of Empires

During the Enlightenment—from the late 17th to the early 19th century, when ideas based on science and reason became important in Europe—thinkers saw that human misery was unwise and even irrational, and they became concerned about the condition of the lower classes. Misery seemed widespread to Europeans in the 18th century, when poor tenant farmers who rented land were often evicted in favor of even cheaper migrant labor or worked very hard by owners who aimed to make as much money as they could. As the Enlightenment spread to the Russian Empire, many of the nobility and even Empress Catherine the Great, who ruled from 1762 to 1796, experimented with new ideas to improve both government and everyday life. In the 1770s and 1780s, the nobleman Alexander Radishchev investigated the condition of the Russian serfs, hoping that his work would lead to some kind of reform. When he tried to publish his book in 1790, government censors would not let it appear. Here is his account of an interview with a serf who is working his plot of rented land on a hot Sunday.

"God help you," I said, walking up to the ploughman, who, without stopping, was finishing the **furrow** he had started. "God help you," I repeated.

< furrow, trench made by a plow for planting seeds

"Thank you, sir," the ploughman said to me, shaking the earth off the **ploughshare** and transferring it to a new furrow. . . .

< ploughshare, the blade of the plow that cuts through the earth

"Have you no time to work during the week, then, and can you not have any rest on Sundays, in the hottest part of the day, at that?"

"In a week, sir, there are six days, and we go six times a week to work on the master's fields; in the evening, if the weather is good, we haul to the master's house the hay that is left in the woods; and on holidays the women and girls go walking in the woods, looking for mushrooms and berries. God grant," he continued, making the sign of the cross, "that it rains this evening. If you have peasants of your own, sir, they are praying to God for the same thing."

"My friend, I have no peasants, and so nobody curses me. Do you have a large family?"

"Three sons and three daughters. The eldest is nine years old."

"But how do you manage to get food enough, if you have only the holidays free?"

"Not only the holidays: the nights are ours, too. If a fellow isn't lazy, he won't starve to death. You see, one horse is resting; and when this one gets tired, I'll take the other; so the work gets done."

"Do you work the same way for your master?"

"No, sir, it would be a sin to work the same way. On his fields there are a hundred hands for one mouth, while I have two for seven mouths; you can figure it out for yourself. No matter how hard you work for the master, no one will thank you for it."

Radishchev's account, *A Journey from St. Petersburg to Moscow,* was translated by Leo Weiner and edited by Roderick Page Thaler (Harvard University Press, 1958). For more background on the history of Russian peasants, see *The Despised and the Damned: The Russian Peasant through the Ages,* by Jules Koslow, (Macmillan, 1972). A scholarly study is *Lord and Peasant in Russia, from the Ninth to the Nineteenth Century,* by Jerome Blum (Princeton University Press, 1961). A history of Russia for younger readers is *Land of Muscovy: The History of Early Russia,* by E. M. Almedingen (Farrar, Straus and Giroux, 1972). Some general adult histories of Russia are *Russia: People and Empire 1552–1917,* by Geoffrey A. Hosking (Harvard University Press, 2001); *Russia: An Illustrated History,* by Joel Carmichael (Hippocrene, 1999); and *Russia: A History,* a beautifully illustrated volume edited by Gregory L. Freeze (Oxford University Press, 2002).

AN AGE OF VOYAGES, 1350–1600

41. Bishops Behaving Badly

ANONYMOUS MANUSCRIPT PAMPHLET, ABOUT 1438

Around the world in the early modern period, monks and religious leaders came under attack from discontented rulers and ordinary people alike. In Europe, long before the monk Martin Luther kicked off the Reformation in 1517, writers criticized the power grabs and wealth of Roman Catholic officials. The following pamphlet, issued by an unknown author before the printing press was invented, worked to undermine the power of the church and turn public opinion against bishops, priests, and even the pope himself. The ultimate result was that people around Europe left the Roman Catholic Church to form new "Protestant" churches.

See chapter 5 of
An Age of Voyages

Concerning the Bishops

Just look at the behavior of today's bishops. They start wars and cause general unrest. They act just like regular princes, which, of course, is what they really are. Instead of being used for honest work in the parish they use the godly donations for this sort of activity— it should not go to finance wars. I think **Duke Frederick** was absolutely right when he told **Emperor Sigismund** at **Basel** that the bishops were blind and it was up to [the princes] to open their eyes. . . .

Duke Frederick, a nobleman; **Emperor Sigismund**, Holy Roman Emperor; **Basel**, city in < Switzerland

Bishops should not own castles. They should live in the main church in their **diocese** and live there like a Christian should. They should be an example to the priests in their diocese. Instead all they

diocese a church district administered < by a bishop

do today is ride about like princes. Peace would stand a better chance if this sort of behavior were abolished. . . .

Everyone knows the harm and suffering caused by giving churches to ignorant, unqualified priests. They cannot preach the Gospel, nor administer the **Sacraments**. We call them "blind guides." If you follow them, you just end up in a ditch.

> Sacraments, holy rites of the Catholic Church

There are several accessible histories of the Reformation: *The Reformation*, by Owen Chadwick (Penguin, 1990); *The Reformation*, by Diarmaid MacCulloch (Viking, 2004); and *The World of the Reformation*, by Hans J. Hillerbrand (Scribner, 1973). *The Reformation: A Narrative History Related by Contemporary Observers and Participants*, also by Hillerbrand (Harper & Row, 1964), draws on many primary sources. *Protestantism*, by Stephen F. Brown (Facts on File, 2002), takes the history of Protestant churches from the Reformation to the present day.

42. The Right Job at the Right Time

MUHAMMAD IBN ASAD JALAL UD-DIN AL-DAWWANI, JALALI'S ETHICS, SECOND HALF OF THE 15TH CENTURY

See chapter 6 of *An Age of Voyages* and chapter 4 of *An Age of Science and Revolutions*

The Persian philosopher Muhammad ibn Asad Jalal ud-din al-Dawwani wrote a popular book called Jalali's Ethics *that explained the proper organization of society. He believed that the various groups in society should be kept in a state of "equipoise"—that is, in balance and harmony. No social group should be dominant over another. All jobs in society had a place and value, and all of them needed to be balanced, just as doctors of the time believed the "four elements"— fire, water, air, and earth—should be in balance in the body.*

The author's ideas seemed so sensible that they gained real influence in India under the Muslim Mughal emperors, and rulers and politicians found the book helpful and persuasive.

> divines, priests;

> exertions, work;
> subsistence, survival

1. *Men of the pen*, such as lawyers, **divines**, judges, bookmen, statisticians, geometricians, astronomers, physicians, poets. In these and their **exertions** in the use of their delightful pens, the **subsistence** of the faith and of the world is . . . bound up. They occupy the place in politics that water does among the elements. Indeed, to persons of

ready understanding, the similarity of knowledge and water is as clear as water itself.

2. *Men of the sword,* such as soldiers, fighting **zealots**, guards of forts and passes, without whose exercise of the **impetuous and vindictive** sword, no arrangement of the age's interests could be effected; without the **havoc** of whose **tempest-like** energies, the materials of corruption, in the shape of rebellious and disaffected persons, could never be dissolved. . . . These then occupy the place of fire. . . .

> **zealots**, fanatics
>
> **impetuous and vindictive**, reckless and spiteful; **havoc**, confusion and disorder; **tempest-like**, like a storm

3. *Men of business,* such as merchants, **capitalists, artisans,** and craftsmen, by whom the means of **emolument** and all other interests are adjusted. . . . The resemblance of these to air—the **auxiliary** of growth and increase in vegetables—the reviver of spirit in animal life . . . is exceedingly **manifest**.

> **capitalists, artisans,** investors, craftspeople; **emolument**, payment for employment; **auxiliary**, helper
>
> **manifest**, obvious

4. *Husbandmen,* such as **seedsmen, bailiffs,** and agriculturalists—the superintendents of vegetation . . . without whose exertions the continuance of humankind must be cut short. These are, in fact, the only producers of what had no previous existence; the other classes . . . only transmitting what subsists already from person to person, from place to place. . . . How close these come to the soil and surface of the earth . . . must be universally apparent.

> **seedsmen, bailiffs,** dealers in seeds and agents of landowners

In like manner then as . . . the passing of any element beyond its proper measure occasions the loss of equipoise, and is followed by **dissolution** and ruin, in political coalition, no less, the prevalence of any one class over the other three. . . . Next attention is to be directed to the condition of the individuals composing them, and the place of every one determined according to his right.

> **dissolution**, falling apart

This selection from *Jalali's Ethics* comes from the standard anthology by William Theodore de Bary, *Sources of the Indian Tradition* (Columbia University Press, 1958).

43. Here Comes the Bride

See chapter 7 of
An Age of Voyages
and chapter 4 of
The European World

*Was there ever a King Arthur? Around 800 CE the Welsh historian
Nennius wrote about a military leader who defeated the invading
Germanic Saxons, and some people think this might be the first story
about King Arthur. Around 1136, Geoffrey of Monmouth, in his*
History of Britain, *told how a great ruler conquered not only all of
Britain but even Europe to the gates of Rome. It all sounds fantastic,
but there is no solid evidence of a real King Arthur. Nor do we know if
there was a Round Table, a wife Guinevere, a lover Launcelot, or a
wizard Merlin, but certainly the legend is alive, thanks especially to
Sir Thomas Malory's* The Death of Arthur. *People know as little
about Thomas Malory as they do about King Arthur.*

*Even so, King Arthur's legend survives today in books and movies,
and the tales of his medieval knights inspire games such as Dungeons
and Dragons. Admirers of President John F. Kennedy likened his time
in office to the brief glory of King Arthur's reign in his court, Camelot.
In this passage, the legendary King Arthur decides to take the lady
Guinevere for his bride.*

In the beginning of Arthur, after he was chosen king by adventure
and by grace; for the most part of the barons knew not that he was

Uther Pendragon, > **Uther Pendragon's** son, but as Merlin made it openly known. But yet
a legendary figure, said many kings and lords made great war against him for that cause, but
to be Arthur's father well Arthur overcame them all, for the most part of the days of his
life he was ruled much by the counsel of Merlin. So it fell on a time

barons, noblemen > King Arthur said unto Merlin, My **barons** will let me have no rest,
but needs I must take a wife, and I will none take but by thy counsel
and by thine advice. It is well done, said Merlin, that ye take a wife,

bounty and noblesse, for a man of your **bounty and noblesse** should not be without a wife.
generosity and nobility > Now is there any that ye love more than another? Yea, said King

Leodegrance, > Arthur, I love Guinevere the king's daughter, **Leodegrance** of the
Guenivere's father; land of **Cameliard**, the which holdeth in his house the Table Round
Cameliard, Gueni- that ye told he had of my father Uther. And this **damosel** is the most
vere's family home; valiant and fairest lady that I know living, or yet that ever I could
damosel, young find. Sir, said Merlin, as of her beauty and fairness she is one of the
unmarried woman

fairest on live, but, an [if] ye loved her not so well as ye do, I should find ye a damosel of beauty and of goodness that should like you and please you, an [if] your heart were not set; but there as a man's heart is set, he will be **loth** to return. That is truth, said King Arthur.

<loth, unwilling

There are countless editions of the King Arthur legend. The version by Thomas Malory is published as *Le Morte d'Arthur* (The Death of Arthur) (Modern Library, 1994, 1999) and in an edition edited by Janet Cowen (Penguin, 1969). The complete *Works* of Malory are available in a single volume, edited by Eugène Vinaver (2nd ed., Oxford University Press, 1977). Excerpts have been published as *King Arthur and His Knights: Selected Tales,* edited by Vinaver (Oxford University Press, 1975), in a handy paperback. An abridged edition of *Le Morte d'Arthur* has been edited by Helen Cooper (Oxford World's Classics, 1998).

There are numerous retellings of the King Arthur stories; for example, *The Acts of King Arthur and his Noble Knights; From the Winchester MMS. of Thomas Malory and Other Sources,* by the novelist John Steinbeck (Farrar, Straus & Giroux, 1976; paperback, Ballantine/Del Rey, 1977). Perhaps the best known, *The Story of King Arthur and His Knights* (1903; reprint, Dover, 1965), was written and illustrated by Howard Pyle. Others designed specifically for young readers are: *King Arthur and the Knights of the Round Table,* by Antonia Fraser (Knopf, 1970); *Of Swords and Sorcerers: The Adventures of King Arthur and his Knights,* by Margaret Hodges (Scribners, 1993); *The Legend of King Arthur,* by Robin Lister (Doubleday, 1990); and *Tales of King Arthur,* by James Riordan (Rand McNally, 1982).

Several writers have debated what is true in the tales and what is not; for example, *Arthur in Fact and Legend,* by Geoffrey Ashe (Thomas Nelson, 1971). In *The World of King Arthur and his Court: People, Places, Legend, and Lore* (Dutton, 1998), Kevin Crossley-Holland surveys the known history of King Arthur, the legends and lore surrounding him, his treatment in literature, and the historical background of the stories. In an earlier book, *The Search for King Arthur* (American Heritage, 1969), Christopher Hibbert and the editors of the magazine *Horizon* discuss real and mythical elements in the Arthurian legend by attempting to identify the historical Arthur and detailing changes in his legend since the sixth century.

44. Ban the Bomb

" DESIDERIUS ERASMUS, LETTER TO ANTHONY OF BERGEN, MARCH 14, 1513

See chapters 4 and 5 of *An Age of Voyages*

Erasmus was one of the great thinkers and religious reformers of his day. A former monk, he was also, like many others in these violent times, opposed to war. He hated the constant fighting among the European states and the war-making of leaders everywhere. In this letter of 1513 to an abbot (the head of a monastery) in France, he pointed out that even animals did not fight each other the way humans did. As a result of these views, he came to dislike the conflict brought about by the Reformation—the movement that challenged the Catholic Church because of its corruption and led to the founding of Protestant churches. Erasmus was a Dutchman who traveled widely, meeting people and writing letters as he moved from city to city. He was part of an expanding of outlooks among Europeans that began in the 16th century.

pitch, height, intensity >

I am frequently amazed as I wonder why it is that men—and I won't call them Christians—are driven to such a **pitch** of madness as to rush into mutual destruction with so much zest and at such tremendous cost and risk. We spend our whole lives fighting wars. Not even animals do that, except wild ones, and they do not battle with their own kind, but only with members of a different species; they fight with the weapons with which nature has provided them, not like us, with war machinery devised by the devil's art. Nor do they fight for any and every reason, but only to protect their young and get food, while our wars, for the most part, are the result of ambition or anger or lust or some such disease of the soul. Finally, animals do not mass together by the thousands, as we do, and then line up to destroy each other. We proudly bear the name of Christ, whose whole life in teaching and example was one of meek-

quickened, made alive; **sacraments**, holy rites of the Catholic Church >

Head, the pope >

supreme union, > mystical union with God after death

ness. For us, who are members of one body, who are one flesh, are **quickened** by the same Spirit, nourished by the same **sacraments**, joined to the same **Head**, called to the same immortal life, and have hopes for that **supreme union** whereby Christ and the Father are one, so that we too may be one with Him—for us, then, can anything in this world be so important as to provoke war? War is so destructive and ugly that, even when it is most just, still it cannot be pleasing to a truly good man. . . .

How many criminal acts are committed **under the guise of** war, since in time of war good laws are silenced! The plundering, the godless conduct . . . and all the other disgraceful things which one would blush to mention! This moral plague must last for several years, even when the war is over.

> **under the guise of,** pretending to be

This letter is printed in *Erasmus and His Age: Selected Letters of Desiderius Erasmus,* edited by Hans J. Hillerbrand and translated by Marcus Haworth (Harper, 1970). *The Erasmus Reader,* edited by Erika Rummel (University of Toronto Press, 1990), provides a helpful selection of Erasmus's writings. Erasmus's major work, *Praise of Folly,* appears in many editions: a translation by Betty Radice (Penguin, 1993); an inexpensive edition of John Wilson's 1668 translation (Dover, 2003); and a new translation by Clarence H. Miller (2nd ed., Yale University Press, 2003). The Norton Critical Edition was edited and translated by Robert M. Adams (Norton, 1989).

A scholarly biography is *Erasmus of Christendom,* by Roland Bainton (Scribners, 1969). *Desiderius Erasmus,* by J. Kelley Sowards, is a useful short biography (Twayne, 1975). A biography for young adults is *Erasmus: The Eye of the Hurricane,* by Charles L. Mee Jr. (Coward, McCann & Geoghegan, 1974).

45. But No Marching Bands

" ALBRECHT DÜRER, JOURNAL OF A TRIP TO THE LOW COUNTRIES, 1520

Early modern people enjoyed many holidays and festivals, and in fact they worked far fewer days than we do today. Religious parades on special holy days brought out people in cities and helped cement them as a community. In 1520, the German artist Albrecht Dürer made a trip through what is now Belgium, then part of the Netherlands, or "Low Countries." He kept a diary while he traveled and was excited about the variety of people that he saw. In the wealthy port city of Antwerp, he watched a parade celebrating the Virgin Mary's Assumption, when she was said to have risen body and soul into heaven—an important holiday for the Roman Catholic Church. His record of the procession shows us who lived in cities in the 16th century and who was considered important.

See chapter 8 of
An Age of Voyages

I saw the great procession from the Church of Our Lady at Antwerp, when the whole town of every craft and **rank** was assembled, each dressed in his best according to his rank. And all ranks and **guilds** had their signs, by which they might be known. In the intervals great costly pole-candles were borne, and their long old **Frankish** trumpets of silver. There were also in the German fashion many pipers and drummers. All the instruments were loudly and noisily blown and beaten.

I saw the procession pass along the street, the people being arranged in rows, each man some distance from his neighbour, but the rows close one behind another. There were the goldsmiths, the

painters, the masons, the **broiderers**, the sculptors, the joiners, the carpenters, the sailors, the fishermen, the butchers, the leatherers, the clothmakers, the bakers, the tailors, the shoemakers—indeed workmen of all kinds, and many craftsmen and dealers who work for their livelihood. Likewise the shopkeepers and merchants and their assistants of all kinds were there. After these came the shooters with guns, bows, and crossbows, and the horsemen and foot-

soldiers also. Then followed a great crowd of the lords **magistrates**. Then came a fine troop all in red, nobly and splendidly clad. Before them, however, went all the religious orders. . . .

A very large company of widows also took part in this procession. They support themselves with their own hands . . . and were all dressed from head to foot in white linen garments, made especially for the occasion. . . .

In this procession very many delightful things were shown, most splendidly got up. Wagons were drawn along with **masques** upon ships and other structures. Among them was the company of the prophets in their order and scenes from the New Testament, such as the **Annunciation**, the Three Holy Kings riding on great camels and on other rare beasts, very well arranged; . . . At the end

came a great dragon, which **St. Margaret** and her maidens led by a **girdle**; she was especially beautiful. Behind her came **St. George** with his squires, a very goodly knight in armor. In this host also rode boys and maidens most finely and splendidly dressed in the costumes of many lands, representing various saints. From beginning to end the procession lasted more than two hours before it was gone by our house.

📖   *The World of Dürer, 1471–1528,* by Francis Russell and the editors of Time-Life Books, a volume in the Time-Life Library of Art (Time-Life Books, 1967), is an excellent introduction to Dürer and his times. Some short illustrated books on Dürer are *Dürer* by Martin Bailey (Phaidon, 1998), *Dürer* by Stefano Zuffi (DK, 1999), and *Albrecht Dürer, 1471–1528* by Anja Eichler (Konemann, 1999). Two scholarly biographies are *Albrecht Dürer: A Biography,* by Jane Campbell Hutchison (Princeton University Press, 1990), and the classic *The Life and Art of Albrecht Dürer,* by Erwin Panofsky (4th ed., Princeton University Press, 1971).

   The Complete Engravings, Etchings, and Drypoints of Albrecht Dürer, edited by Walter L. Strauss (Dover, 1972), and *The Complete Woodcuts of Albrecht Dürer,* edited by Willi Kurth (Dover, 1963), are useful and well-priced books of the artist's work. A similar volume is *The Complete Drawings of Albrecht Dürer,* edited by Walter L. Strauss (Abaris, 1974).

46. Ideas about Women—Some of Them New

❝ MARTIN LUTHER, TABLE TALK, 1530s

Martin Luther was a German monk who broke with the Roman Catholic Church over the selling of indulgences—certificates that claimed to shorten the time a soul spent in Purgatory, waiting to get into Heaven. He established himself as the head of a reformed "Lutheran" faith in the university town of Wittenberg (in present-day eastern Germany), often holding forth at the dinner table to his family and a long series of visitors. Some visitors to his home collected his opinions into a popular book later published as Table Talk. *In this collection, Luther offered his private, often humorous and irreverent thoughts on a wide variety of subjects, such as the position of women in society. In addressing this topic, he differed yet again with the Catholic Church, many of whose important thinkers maintained that it was less godly to marry than to remain single.*

See chapter 5 of *An Age of Voyages*

Between June 12 and July 12, 1532. Many good things may be perceived in a wife. First there is the Lord's blessing, namely, off-spring. Then there is **community** of property. These are some of the preeminently good things that can overwhelm a man.

< community, sharing

Imagine what it would be like without this sex. The home, cities, economic life and government would virtually disappear. Men can't do without women. Even if it were possible for men to **beget and bear** children, they still couldn't do without women.

beget and bear, to >
father and mother

Between December 11, 1532 and January 2, 1533. Female government has never done any good. God made Adam master over all creatures, to rule over all living things, but when Eve persuaded him that he was lord even over God she spoiled everything. We have you women to thank for that! With tricks and cunning women deceive men, as I, too, have experienced.

Mantua, community in
northern Italy where
a Catholic Church
council was meeting >

celibacy, the Catholic >
Church requires that
priests be celibate, that
is, unmarried

Between January 13 and 31, 1537. Martin Luther looked admiringly at a painting of his wife and said, "I think I'll have a husband added to that painting, send it to **Mantua** and inquire whether they prefer marriage [to **celibacy**]."

Then he began to speak in praise of marriage, the divine institution from which everything proceeds and without which the whole world would have remained empty and all creatures would have been meaningless and of no account, since they were created for the sake of man.... Since [Adam] defines and praises [marriage] it is only right that we put a **charitable construction** on everything that may be frail in a woman.

charitable >
construction,
positive spin

November 4, 1538. A certain Englishman, a learned man, sat at the table and could not understand the German language. Luther said "I recommend my wife to you as a teacher of the German language. She's very fluent. She's such a ready speaker that she's much better at it than I am. However, eloquence in women shouldn't be praised; it's more fitting for them to lisp and stammer. This is more becoming to them.

The full text of *Table Talk* is published as volume 54 of *Luther's Works*, edited by Theodore G. Tappert (Fortress Press, 1967). Selections from those texts are in *Conversations with Luther: Selections from Recently Published Sources of the Table Talk*, translated and edited by Preserved Smith and Herbert Percival Gallinger (1915; reprint, Keats, 1979). Writings on the same subject are collected in *Luther on Women: A Sourcebook*, edited and translated by Susan C. Karant-Nunn and Merry E. Wiesner-Hanks (Cambridge University Press, 2003). Two other collections of Luther's writings are *Selected Writings of Martin Luther,* edited by Theodore G. Tappert (Fortress Press, 1967), and *Martin Luther's Basic Theological Writings,* edited by Timothy F. Lull (Fortress Press, 1989).

A recent short biography, part of the Penguin Lives series, is *Martin Luther,* by Martin E. Marty (Penguin, 2004). *Martin Luther: An Illustrated Biography,* by Peter Manns (Crossroad, 1983), Sally Stepanek's *Martin Luther* (Chelsea House, 1986), and Samuel Crompton's *Martin Luther* (Chelsea House, 2003) are three biographies for young adults. *Martin Luther,* by Judith O'Neill (Lerner, 1979), is a short biography for younger readers.

47. Bashfulness—Getting Over It

" **JOHN CALVIN, COMMENTARIES ON THE BOOK OF PSALMS, 1557**

Jean Calvin lived during a time of great violence between Catholics and Protestants. The Catholic French king at first tolerated Protestants but then changed his mind and began a policy of imprisoning and even executing them. Calvin, a French Protestant, ran for his life in the 1530s to Geneva, Switzerland, where Protestants were safer than they were in Paris or other parts of France. Calvin quickly made himself head of an international Protestant church with branches not only in France but also in Britain, where he was commonly known as John, the English form of Jean. This autobiographical story, which Calvin inserted in one of his biblical commentaries, explains how he turned his rebelliousness into leadership—with God's help. Other Protestants, influenced by Martin Luther, Calvin, and other Protestant leaders, wrote their own life stories about how and why they changed their religious faith.

See chapter 5 of *An Age of Voyages*

[Just] as [the biblical King David] was taken from the **sheepfold** and elevated to the rank of supreme authority, so God having taken me from my originally obscure and humble condition has reckoned me worthy of being invested with the honorable office of a preacher and minister of the gospel. When I was as yet a very little boy, my father had destined me for the study of **theology**. But afterwards, when he considered that the legal profession commonly raised those who followed it to wealth, this prospect **induced** him suddenly to change

< **sheepfold,** pen for sheep; David began as a shepherd boy

< **theology,** religious thought

< **induced,** caused

his purpose. Thus it came to pass that I was withdrawn from the study of philosophy and was put to the study of law. To this pursuit I endeavored faithfully to apply myself, in obedience to the will of my father; but God, by the secret guidance of His **providence**, at length gave a different direction to my course. And first, since I was too obstinately devoted to the **superstitions of popery** to be easily extricated. . . . God by a sudden conversion subdued and brought my mind to a teachable frame. . . . Having thus received some taste and knowledge of true godliness, I was immediately inflamed with so intense a desire to make progress therein, that although I did not altogether leave off other studies, I yet pursued them with less **ardor**.

I was quite surprised to find that before a year had elapsed, all who had any desire after **purer doctrine** were continually coming to me to learn, although I myself was as yet but a mere novice and **tyro**. Being of a **disposition** somewhat unpolished and bashful, which led me always to love the shade and retirement, I then began to seek some secluded corner where I might be withdrawn from the public view; but so far from being able to accomplish the object of my desire, all my retreats were like public schools. In short, whilst my one great object was to live in seclusion without being known, God so led me about through different turnings and changes that He never permitted me to rest in any place, until, in spite of my natural disposition, He brought me forth to public notice.

providence, divine > guidance

superstitions of popery, Catholic rites, which Protestants, who rejected the pope's authority, believed were founded on superstition, not true faith; **ardor,** passion

purer doctrine, > Christianity based on the Bible alone; **tyro,** beginner; **disposition,** personality, character

David W. Torrance and Thomas F. Torrance have edited *Calvin's Commentaries* (Eerdmans, 1959). Some of his other writings are available in *John Calvin: Writings on Pastoral Piety,* edited and with translations by Elsie Anne McKee (Paulist Press, 2001).

There are two biographies for young adults: *John Calvin* by Sally Stepanek (Chelsea House, 1986) and *John Calvin* by Thomas J. Davis (Chelsea House, 2004). There are quite a few scholarly biographies: *John Calvin: A Sixteenth-century Portrait,* by William J. Bouwsma (Oxford University Press, 1988); *Calvin: A Biography,* by Bernard Cottret (Eerdmans, 2000); *A Life of John Calvin: A Study of the Shaping of Western Culture,* by Alister E. McGrath (Blackwell, 1990). See also *Calvin: An Introduction to His Thought,* by T. H. L. Parker (Continuum, 2002). A useful reference book (actually a collection of essays) is *The Cambridge Companion to John Calvin,* edited by Donald K. McKim (Cambridge University Press, 2004).

48. An Ideal Renaissance Man

LAUNOY, HISTORY OF THE COLLEGE OF NAVARRE IN PARIS, 1667

During the Renaissance, Europeans began to value accomplishments and not just good, religious behavior that would get them into heaven. People were noticed for doing practical things and being skilled in many activities. Here is the legendary story set down by a little-known author in a 17th-century Latin history of a secondary school, the College of Navarre, about a true "Renaissance man," Fernando of Cordova in Spain, who could do everything well. Fernando arrived at the College of Navarre in Paris in 1445, amazing people and even making some suspect that he was somehow given his gifts by the devil. There have been other noted "Renaissance men," including important Americans such as Benjamin Franklin and Thomas Jefferson. Both men knew how to do many things, such as plan gardens, do architecture, carry out scientific experiments, and serve as diplomats and politicians.

See chapter 2 of
An Age of Voyages

In the year 1445 there came to the College of Navarre a certain youth of twenty summers who was **past master** of all good arts, as the most skilled masters of the university testified with one accord. He sang beautifully to the flute: he surpassed all in numbers, voice, **modes**, and symphony. He was a painter and laid colours on images best of all. In military matters he was most expert: he swung a sword with both hands so well and mightily that none dared fight with him. No sooner did he **espy** his foe he would leap at him with one spring from a distance of twenty or twenty-four feet. He was a master in arts, in medicine, in **both laws**, in theology. With us in the school of Navarre he engaged in **disputation**, although we numbered more than fifty of the most perfect masters. I omit three thousand others and more who attended the bout. So shrewdly and cumulatively did he reply to all the questions which were proposed that he surpassed the belief, if not of those present, certainly of those absent. Latin, Greek, Hebrew, Arabic, and many more tongues he spoke in a most polished manner. He was a very skilful horseman. Nay more, if any man should live to be a hundred and pass days and sleepless nights without food and drink, he would never acquire the

< **past master,** someone who has completely mastered his craft

< **modes,** musical system similar to scales

< **espy,** see, lay eyes on

< **both laws,** canon, or church, law and civil law; **disputation,** formal debate

knowledge which that lad's mind embraced. And indeed he filled us with deep awe, for he knew more than human nature can bear.

📖 For other primary sources from the Renaissance, see *The Italian Renaissance Reader,* by Julia Conaway Bondanella and Mark Musa (Plume, 1987). Jonathan W. Zophy offers a brief introduction to the Renaissance covering the major personalities, issues, events, and ideas of the period, *A Short History of Renaissance and Reformation Europe: Dances over Fire and Water,* 3d ed. (Prentice-Hall, 2002). Theodore K. Rabb's *Renaissance Lives: Portrait of an Age* (Basic Books, 2001) provides 15 biographies, each illustrating a different aspect of the time.

49. Be Scary, Be Very Scary

❝ NICCOLÒ MACHIAVELLI, THE PRINCE, 1532

See chapter 2 of
An Age of Voyages

Niccolò Machiavelli was a lawyer's son who grew up in Florence in the 15th century, when the wealthy and powerful Lorenzo de' Medici governed the Italian city. In the Florentine Republic, Machiavelli served as a counselor with a special interest in military affairs and as a diplomat. In 1513 the city's leaders came to suspect that Machiavelli was part of a conspiracy against the Medicis and sent him into enforced retirement for the rest of his life. In exile, he wrote histories and essays, especially The Prince, *his advice book on being an effective ruler, which was published after his death, in 1532. Unlike other books that urged princes to be virtuous and pious, Machiavelli's concentrated on the realities of political power.*

In the following passage, Machiavelli answers the age-old question of whether a prince should rule through being loved or being feared by his subjects. He says the prince must be prepared to imitate the strategies of animals, combining the lion's strength and the fox's cunning. Machiavelli's Prince *became an important guide for rulers in the modern age. Even though many criticized Machiavelli's ideas as ruthless, the same people might secretly have followed the practical advice his book offered.*

Cesare Borgia,
powerful Italian lord >

Every prince must desire to be considered merciful and not cruel. He must, however, take care not to misuse this mercifulness. **Cesare Borgia** was considered cruel, but his cruelty had brought order to the **Romagna,** united it, and reduced it to peace and **fealty.** . . . A < Romagna, region in northern Italy; **fealty,** allegiance

prince, therefore, must not mind incurring the charge of cruelty for the purpose of keeping his subjects united and faithful; for, with a very few examples, he will be more merciful than those who, from excess of tenderness, allow disorders to arise, from whence spring bloodshed and **rapine**; for these as a rule injure the whole commu- < rapine, robbery

nity, while the executions carried out by the prince injure only individuals. . . .

From this arises the question whether it is better to be loved more than feared, or feared more than loved. The reply is, that one ought to be both feared and loved, but as it is difficult for the two to go together, it is much safer to be feared than loved, if one of the two has to be wanting. For it may be said of men in general that they are ungrateful, **voluble, dissemblers,** anxious to avoid danger, < voluble, dissemblers, noisy liars; **covetous of gain,** greedy; **have less scruple in,** are less worried about

and **covetous of gain.** . . . Men **have less scruple in** offending one who makes himself loved than one who makes himself feared.

Still, a prince should make himself feared in such a way that if he does not gain love, he at any rate avoids hatred; for fear and the absence of hatred may well go together, and will always be attained by one who abstains from interfering with the property of his citizens and subjects. . . .

How **laudable** it is for a prince to keep good faith and live with < laudable, praiseworthy; **astuteness,** slyness

integrity and not with **astuteness,** everyone knows. Still the experience of our times shows those princes to have done great things who have had little regard for good faith, and have been able by astuteness to confuse men's brains. . . .

You must know, then, that there are two methods of fighting, the one by law, the other by force: the first method is that of men, the second of beasts; but as the first method is often insufficient, one must have recourse to the second. It is therefore necessary for a prince to know well how to use both the beast and the man. . . .

A prince being thus obliged to know well how to act as a beast must imitate the fox and the lion, for the lion cannot protect himself from traps, and the fox cannot defend himself from wolves. One must therefore be a fox to recognize traps, and a lion to frighten wolves. Those that wish to be only lions do not understand this.

There are numerous modern translations and editions of *The Prince*: a translation by George Bull, with an introduction by the Princeton historian Anthony Grafton, in the Penguin Classics series (Penguin, 2003); the Norton Critical Edition, by Robert M. Adams (2nd ed., Norton, 1992); a translation by Mark Musa (St. Martin's, 1964); another by W. K. Marriot, in Everyman's Library (Knopf, 1992); an edition by Peter Bondanella and Mark Musa in the Oxford World's Classics series (Oxford University Press, 1984). A new translation is by political scientist Harvey Mansfield (University of Chicago Press, 1985). There is also an inexpensive translation by N. H. Thomson (Dover, 1992).

For a biography of Macchiavelli, see *Niccolo's Smile: A Biography of Machiavelli*, by Maurizio Viroli and translated by Antony Shugaar (Farrar, Straus & Giroux, 2002). *Machiavelli: A Very Short Introduction*, by Quentin Skinner (Oxford University Press, 2000) is a primer on Machiavelli's philosophy.

50. A Cranky Pilgrim, a Boastful Monkey, and Pigsy

WU CHENG'EN, JOURNEY TO THE WEST, 1592

See chapter 3 of
An Age of Voyages
and chapter 2 of
The Asian World

In 1592, the great Chinese epic Journey to the West *(sometimes called* Monkey *after one of its main characters) was published. The epic retells the story of the legendary Buddhist pilgrim Xuanzang, who lived during the Tang dynasty (618–906 CE). Its probable author was Wu Cheng'en, about whom we know very little except that he lived from 1505 to 1580. The author took great liberties with the life of the pilgrim, who had traveled across Asia to increase his faith and to find sacred Buddhist books to bring back to China. In the book, the pilgrim has become crabby and is a scaredy-cat who is terrified of sounds, animals, and even ordinary people.*

The real hero of the story is the pilgrim's guide—an irreverent, adventurous monkey who has gained enlightenment and learned to perform many magic feats even before he meets the pilgrim. Monkey boastfully calls himself "Great Sage Equal to Heaven"—a name that suggests that he is equal to the gods and to the Chinese emperor, who was said to rule with the approval of heaven. The story shows that Monkey, for all his talents, is constantly in trouble, often because his own pride keeps him from learning his lessons well enough. Monkey is now a popular cartoon character in East Asia.

In this part of the story, a hoglike monster called Pigsy helps Monkey escort the pilgrim on his quest to find sacred books. They are fighting a river monster called Sandy who is keeping the monk from crossing a vast river, the River of Flowing Sands, on his way to India. The monster keeps diving into the water to escape Monkey and Pigsy, who report their momentary failure to the pilgrim. In this part of the story, the pilgrim is called by an Indian name, Tripitaka.

Tripitaka burst into tears. "We shall never get across," he sobbed. "Don't you worry," said Monkey. "It is true that with that creature lying in wait for us, we can't get across. But Pigsy, you stay here by the Master and don't attempt to do any more fighting. I'm going off to the Southern Ocean." "And what are you going to do there?" asked Pigsy. "This scripture-seeking business" said Monkey, "is an invention of the **Bodhisattva**, and it was she who converted us. It is surely for her to find some way of getting us over this river. I'll go and ask her. It's a better idea than fighting with the monster." ...

> **Bodhisattva,** enlightened being who delays achieving perfection in order to help others

Monkey somersaulted into the clouds, and in less than half an hour he had reached the Southern Ocean and saw **Mount Potalaka** rise before him. After landing he went straight to the Purple Bamboo Grove. ... The Bodhisattva was leaning against the **parapet** of the Lotus Pool, looking at the flowers. ... "Why aren't you looking after your master?" she said to Monkey, when he was brought in. "When we came to the River of Flowing Sands," said Monkey, "we found it guarded by a monster formidable in the arts of war." ... "You obstinate ape," said the Bodhisattva, "this is the same thing all over again. Why didn't you say that you were in charge of the priest of T'ang?" "We were both far too busy trying to catch him and make him take the Master across," said Monkey. "I put him there on purpose to help scripture-seekers," said **Kuan-yin**.

> **Mount Potalaka,** a mythical home of divine beings; **parapet,** low wall

> **Kuan-yin,** Chinese name for Bodhisattva Guayin, also spelled Kwan-yin

Monkey returns to the river, determined to follow the Bodhisattva's advice, not his own pride. With the guide Hui-yen and Pigsy, Monkey announces himself to the monster Sandy, with whom he has been fighting.

"Well," said Sandy, looking at Pigsy, "that filthy creature never said a word about scriptures, though I fought with him for two days." Then seeing Monkey, "What is that fellow there too?" he cried. "He's the other's partner. I'm not going near them." "The first is Pigsy," said Hui-yen, "and the second is Monkey. They are both Tripitaka's disciples. . . . I myself will introduce you to the Master." Sandy put away his staff, tidied himself and scrambled to the bank. When they reached Tripitaka, Sandy knelt before him, exclaiming "How can I have been so blind as not to recognize you? Forgive me for all my rudeness!"

brazen, bold, > "You **brazen** creature," said Pigsy, "why did you insist on having a row
shameless with us, instead of joining our party from the start?" "Brother," laughed Monkey, "don't scold him. It is we who are to blame, for never having told him that we were going to get scriptures." "Is it indeed your earnest desire to dedicate yourself to our religion?" asked Tripitaka. Sandy bowed his assent, and Tripitaka told Monkey to take a knife and shave his head. . . . Tripitaka thought that Sandy shaped very well as a priest and was thoroughly satisfied with him.

The translation used here is by Arthur Waley, and is published as *Monkey* (Unwin, 1942, 1984; Grove Press, 1984). Another translation is by W. J. F. Jenner (Foreign Languages Press, 1990). There is a new four-volume edition for scholars by Anthony C. Yu, published as *The Journey to the West* (University of Chicago Press, 1977–83). A shorter version by David Kherdian is *Monkey: A Journey to the West* (Shambhala, 1992).

There are several illustrated retellings of the Monkey stories for children: *Monkey King*, by Ed Young (HarperCollins, 2001); *Monkey King Wreaks Havoc in Heaven*, by Debby Chen (Pan Asian Publications, 2001); *Monkey and the Three Wizards*, translated by Peter Harris and illustrated by Michael Foreman (Bradbury Press, 1977).

AN AGE OF SCIENCE AND REVOLUTIONS, 1600–1800

51. Man of La Mancha

MIGUEL DE CERVANTES, DON QUIXOTE, 1605

Don Quixote, one of the great characters in European literature, was a crazy scholar who dreamed of being a knight in shining armor like those he loved to read about. His creator, Miguel de Cervantes, was a 16th-century Spanish novelist, poet, and playwright and one of the first authors to try, in the new age of the printing press, to make a living by writing books. He was not at all successful, but during his adventurous life as a soldier and even as a slave rowing in a galley (a type of ship), he managed to produce a wide variety of works, including one of the most renowned books in Western literature. Don Quixote *gives a comic view of Spanish society at the end of its "golden age," when Spanish explorers and soldiers conquered rich lands in the Americas and elsewhere and when Spain's literary and artistic cultures reached a high point. The story remained so appealing through the centuries that in the 1970s it was made into the popular musical* Man of La Mancha.

The novel concerns the adventures of an aging warrior, Don Quixote de la Mancha, who has been driven almost insane by reading too many romances about knights and chivalry, the knights' code of honor. Under this influence Don Quixote sets out, with his faithful peasant companion Sancho Panza, on a mission to fulfill his imagined knightly ideals and to improve the world. The world is more complicated than we think, Cervantes seems to tell us, and dreams of knighthood have no place there. Behaving like a knight is fanciful, crazy, or

See chapter 9 of *An Age of Empires* and chapter 2 of *An Age of Voyages simply "quixotic"—a word meaning extravagant or impractical that comes from the character's name.*

They caught sight of thirty or forty windmills standing on the plain, and as soon as Don Quixote saw them he said to his **squire**:

squire, knight's attendant

"Fortune is directing our affairs even better than we could have wished: for you can see over there, good friend Sancho Panza, a place where stand thirty or more monstrous giants with whom I intend to fight a battle and whose lives I intend to take; and with the **booty** we shall begin to prosper. For this is a just war, and it is a great service to God to wipe such a wicked breed from the face of the earth."

booty, goods taken during wartime

"What giants?" said Sancho Panza.

"Those giants that you can see over there," replied his master, "with long arms: there are giants with arms almost six miles long."

"Look you here," Sancho retorted, "those over there aren't giants, they're windmills and what look to you like arms are sails—when the wind turns them they make the millstones go round."

"It is perfectly clear," replied Don Quixote, "that you are but a raw **novice** in this matter of adventures. They are giants; and if you are frightened, you can take yourself away and say your prayers while I engage them in fierce and **arduous** combat."

novice, beginner

arduous, difficult

And so saying he set spurs to his steed Rocinante, not paying any attention to his squire Sancho Panza, who was shouting that what he was charging were definitely windmills, not giants. But Don Quixote was so convinced that they were giants that he neither heard his squire Sancho's shouts nor saw what stood in front of him, even though he was by now upon them; instead he cried:

"Flee not, O vile and cowardly creatures, for it is but one solitary knight who attacks you."

A gust of wind arose, the great sails began to move, and Don Quixote yelled: "Though you flourish more arms than the giant **Briareus**, I will make you pay for it."

Briareus, giant in a medieval romance

So saying, and commending himself with all his heart to his lady Dulcinea, begging her to **succour** him in his plight, well protected by his little round infantryman's shield, and with his

succour, help

lance couched, he advanced at Rocinante's top speed and charged at the windmill nearest him. As he thrust his lance into its sail the wind turned it with such violence that it smashed the lance into pieces and dragged the horse and his rider with it, and Don Quixote went rolling over the plain in a very sore predicament.

< lance couched, long wooden-handled spear lowered to the position for attacking, or charging

There are many editions of the full text of *Don Quixote*: translated and edited by Walter Starkie (Signet, 1971); translated by Tobias Smollett, with an introduction by Carlos Fuentes and notes by Stephanie Kirk (Modern Library, 2001); translated by Charles Jarvis, with an introduction by Milan Kundera, in the Oxford World's Classics series (Oxford University Press, 1999); and translated by Edith Grossman, with an introduction by Harold Bloom (Ecco, 2003). The Norton Critical Edition is translated by Burton Raffel and edited by Diana de Armas Wilson (Norton, 1999).

For biographies of the author, see the brief *Cervantes,* by P. E. Russell (Oxford University Press, 1985), and the young adult biography *Miguel de Cervantes,* by Jake Goldberg (Chelsea House, 1993).

There are many retellings for young people, including the classic *The Adventures of Don Quixote de la Mancha,* by Leighton Barret, illustrated with drawings by Warren Chappell (Knopf, 1939); *Don Quixote and Sancho Panza,* by Margaret Hodges (Scribner, 1992); *Don Quixote and the Windmills,* by Eric A. Kimmel, with pictures by Leonard Everett Fisher (Farrar, Straus & Giroux, 2004); *The Knight and the Squire,* by Argentina Palacios (Doubleday, 1979); and *Exploits of Don Quixote,* by James Reeves, illustrated by Edward Ardizzone (1959; Peter Bedrick, 1985).

52. Go, Team!

YANG SZU-CH'ANG, "DRAGON BOAT RACE," ABOUT 1630

People in early modern times enjoyed many festivals and public games that included sports. The festivals were often religious celebrations, and the games could feature such contests as races and fights between roosters. The dragon boat race, described by Yang Szu-ch'ang—a Chinese man who wrote essays during the late Ming dynasty—was a combined festival, religious observance, and contest among rival teams of rowers. The races, honoring an ancient Chinese poet who drowned on the day they were held, used boats made with the features of a dragon. Yang explains the people's enthusiasm for both the race and its religious significance. They followed many rules

See chapter 5 of *An Age of Science and Revolutions,* chapter 3 of *An Age of Voyages,* and chapter 12 of *The Asian World for proper behavior before and during the race and at the same time became wild with emotions that lingered long after the race was over. Like festivals in other parts of the world, this race, which took place in the Hunan region of China in our month of June, brought people together and gave them a little break from the difficult work life that most of them led.*

avert, prevent, ward > off; **paper coins,** imitation coins with symbolic significance

The current popular belief is that the boat race is held to **avert** misfortunes. At the end of the race, the boats carry sacrificial animals, wine, and **paper coins** and row straight downstream, where the animals and wine are cast into the water, the paper coins are burned,

spells, words believed > to have magic power; **pestilence,** epidemic disease; **premature death,** death before old age

and the **spells** are recited. The purpose of these acts is to make **pestilence** and **premature death** flow away in the water. . . . Then the boats row back without flags and drum-beating. They will be pulled onto land and housed in huts on the shore till the next year, as this year's races are over. About this time the people have rites performed to ward off fires. Also, those who are ill make paper boats in the same color as the dragon boat of their region and burn them at the shore. . . .

The man chosen as the headman of a racing boat must be brave and have a family. Several days before, he distributes steamed cakes and pieces of paper to those who belong to his region and is repaid in money. On the top of the pieces of paper pictures of dragon boats are printed and on the bottom some sentences are written.

Supplying food and wine during the race is assigned to rich men, who are honored if they contribute generously. Others supply food because they have made a vow to do so. On the day of the races there are small boats in the river bringing food. They are decorated with two trees of paper money and colored silks, and musicians play in them. The boatmen must force in the food and wine

satiation, being full >

beyond the point of **satiation** until nothing is left. Otherwise anything left has to be thrown into the water together with the dishes and chopsticks.

In the evening when the boats return, the people take the water

purification, ritual cleansing >

in the boats, mix it with various grasses, and use it to wash their bodies. This is said to prevent bad luck and is a kind of **purification.**

People watch the boat races from the shore. . . . When the start of the race is announced, everyone stops talking, laughing or leaning against the **balustrades**. Attentively they watch, wondering < balustrades, railings which is their boat and whether it will meet victory or defeat. All too quickly victory is decided. Then some are so proud it seems as if their spirits could break the ceiling, and some have faces pale as death and seem not to know how to go down the stairs. . . .

The victorious boat rows with its **stern** forward. The men hold < stern, back of a boat their oars vertically, dance, and beat gongs on the boat. When they pass a losing boat, they threaten it. Those losing try to do the same but with less spirit, or if a little further behind, they silently acknowledge defeat. . . . At the home of the headmen, feasts are prepared and the boatmen all gather to dine. At the victor's home, food and wine are especially abundant, and his neighbors, relatives, and friends come to offer congratulations. The next day, the door of his house will be beautifully decorated with colored silk, and a feast and a dramatic performance will be held. Some people write sentences or short poems on the city gates to ridicule the losers, or tie up a dog or a tortoise with some grass and fruit and place them there for the same purpose. When the men of the defeated boats happen to pass by, they lower their heads and go on their way. . . .

From the fourth month the people begin to talk enthusiastically about the boats. In the fifth month the race is held and victory and defeat are decided. Yet even by the eighth or ninth month the people are still not tired of the subject.

Mooncakes and Hungry Ghosts: Festivals of China, by Carol Stepanchuk (China Books & Periodicals, 1991), is an excellent overview of traditional celebrations. *Awakening the Dragon,* by Arlene Chan (Tundra Books, 2004), is a picture book about the traditional dragon boat festival. *Moonbeams, Dumplings, and Dragon Boats: A Treasury of Chinese Holiday Tales, Activities, and Recipes,* by Nina Simonds, Leslie Swartz, and the Children's Museum of Boston (Gulliver Books/Harcourt, 2002), is a rich source of activities and literature.

53. Burning Down the House

"

SAMUEL PEPYS, DIARY, 1666

See chapter 10 of
*An Age of Science
and Revolutions*

*Around the world, fire was a more devastating event in medieval and
early modern times than it is today. Houses were made of materials
such as wood and thatch, or reeds, that burned easily, and the only
equipment available for putting out a fire was buckets of water. So
when a city started to burn, there was a good chance that hundreds if
not thousands of houses would be destroyed. Samuel Pepys, who
worked for the English government, wrote a lively diary of his life. It
includes an account of the disastrous "Great London Fire" of 1666,
which destroyed much of the city over several days. The fire was so
fierce that the authorities ordered some of the close-packed buildings
to be blown up with gunpowder, creating a space and preventing the
blaze from spreading from house to house. Pepys's diary was later
published, because it provides a vivid account of historic events as
well as a picture of everyday life in 17th-century London—a time of
both science and revolution in the city.*

Lord's Day, Sunday > September 2nd (**Lord's Day**). Some of our maids sitting up late last
night . . . called us up about three in the morning, to tell us of a great
fire they saw in the City. So I rose, and slipped on my night-gown, and
went to her window; and thought it to be on the back-side of Market-
lane at the farthest, but being unused to such fires as followed, I
thought it far enough off; and so went to bed again, and to sleep.
About seven rose again to dress myself, and there looked out at the
window, and saw the fire not so much as it was, and further off. . . .

lamentable, terrible > I [walked] down to the water-side, and there . . . saw a **lamentable**
fire. . . . Every body endeavouring to remove their goods, and flinging

lighter, small boat > into the river, or bringing them into **lighters** that lay off; poor people
used to move cargo
to shore

staying in their houses as long as till the very fire touched them, and
then running into boats, or clambering from one pair of stairs by the
water-side to another. . . . Having stayed, and in an hour's time seen
the fire rage every way, and nobody, to my sight endeavouring to
quench it, but to remove their goods, and leave all to the fire, and

Steele-yard, possibly > having seen it get as far as the **Steele-yard**, and the wind mighty high,
a tavern

and driving it into the City: and every thing after so long a drought proving combustible, even the very stones of the churches. . . . At last met my Lord Mayor in Canning-street, like a man **spent**, with a < spent, exhausted handkerchief about his neck ... he cried, like a fainting woman, "Lord! what can I do? I am spent: people will not obey me. I have been pulling down houses; but the fire overtakes us faster than we can do it." . . .

[September] 4th. . . . Now begins the practice of blowing up of houses in Tower-street, those next the Tower, which at first did frighten people more than anything; but it stopped the fire where it was done, it bringing down the houses to the ground in the same places they stood, and then it was easy to quench what little fire was in it, though it kindled nothing almost.

There are many modern editions of the diary of Samuel Pepys: the Everyman's Library volume, edited by John Warrington (Dutton, 1953); an edition by Mynors Bright and Henry Wheatley (Random House, 1946); another by Richard Le Gallienne, with an introduction by Robert Louis Stevenson (Modern Library, 2001); a new and complete transcription in 11 volumes edited by Robert Latham, William Matthews, and others (University of California Press, 1970-83). Selections from this last edition are published both as *The Illustrated Pepys: Extracts from the Diary* (University of California Press, 1978) and *A Pepys Anthology: Passages from the Diary of Samuel Pepys* (University of California Press, 1988).

There are also several biographies, including *Samuel Pepys: A Life,* by Stephen Coote (Palgrave, 2001), and *Samuel Pepys: The Unequalled Self,* by the distinguished English literary biographer Claire Tomalin (Knopf, 2002). *Samuel Pepys* is a short biography for students by Ivan E. Taylor (Twayne, 1989). *Samuel Pepys and His World,* by Geoffrey Trease (Putnam, 1972), is a concise illustrated biography.

54. Doing the New Science

COUNT LORENZO MAGALOTTI, TRAVELS OF COSMO, GRAND DUKE OF TUSCANY, 1669

Individual thinkers brought about the early modern advances in science, including discoveries in astronomy, physics, and biology, known as the Scientific Revolution. But groups of people coming together to discuss the latest discoveries also played a big part in the new science. These

See chapter 6 of
An Age of Science and Revolutions

groups were called academies or scientific societies, and they formed mostly in important European cities such as Paris and London. The king or queen often officially sponsored these groups, making them royal academies or societies. People interested in science often traveled great distances to attend their meetings, because the academies were an important way for people to learn about the newest finds in science, and because they kept their own collections of objects such as stuffed rare birds. These collections were housed in special rooms called "cabinets of curiosities," a name that captures the wonder with which people looked at all the new discoveries coming in from around the world. The "curiosities" sometimes included exhibits of humans—such as preserved bodies, body parts, or even living people.

In the long run, scientific societies helped inventors and researchers in their work, because they formed a tight network where the members could safely share ideas that might otherwise offend people who feared that science would upset old beliefs, especially religious ones. People also admired the societies because their members agreed to behave with good manners and respect one another during meetings. Count Lorenzo Magalotti, an Italian nobleman traveling with Cosmo, the Grand Duke of Tuscany, left this eyewitness account of his visit to the Royal Society in London in 1669.

At their meetings no . . . distinction of place is observed, except by the president and secretary. The first is in the middle of the table, and the latter at the head of it, on his left hand, the other academicians taking their seats indifferently on benches of wood with backs to them arranged in two rows. And if anyone enters unexpectedly after the meeting has begun everyone remains seated, nor is his **salutation** returned except by the president alone, who acknowledges it by an **inclination** of the head, that he may not interrupt the person who is speaking on the subject or experiment proposed by the secretary. They observe the ceremony of . . . explaining their sentiments in few words relative to the subject under discussion; and to avoid confusion and disorder one does not begin before the other has ended his speech. Neither are opposite opinions maintained with **obstinacy**, but with **temper**, the language of civility and moderation being always adopted amongst them, which renders them so much more praise-worthy as they are a society composed of persons of different nations.

salutation, greeting

inclination, tilt or nod

obstinacy, stubbornness; temper, calmness

The cabinet ... is full of the greatest rarities, brought from the most distant parts, such as **quadrupeds**, birds, fishes, serpents, insects, shells, feathers, seeds, minerals, and many **petrifications**, mummies, and **gums.** And every day, in order to enrich it still more, the academicians contribute everything of value which comes into their hands, so that in time it will be the most beautiful, the largest, and the most curious in respect of natural productions that is anywhere to be found. Amongst these curiosities the most remarkable are an ostrich whose young were always born alive, an herb which grew in the stomach of a **thrush**, and the skin of a **Moor, tanned,** with the beard and hair white. But more worthy of observation than all the rest is a clock whose movements are derived from the vicinity of a **loadstone**; and it is so adjusted as to discover the distance of countries at sea by the longitude.

< **quadrupeds**, four-legged animals; **petrifications**, fossils; **gum**, hardened tree sap

< **thrush**, a small songbird; **Moor, tanned**, North African Arab, preserved in the manner of leather; **loadstone**, magnet (now spelled "lodestone")

There are several scholarly accounts of the Royal Society in London: *The Royal Society: Concept and Creation,* by Margery Purver (MIT Press, 1967); *Women, Science, and Medicine 1500-1700: Mothers and Sisters of the Royal Society,* edited by Lynette Hunter and Sarah Hutton (Sutton, 1997); and *The Royal Society, 1660-1940: A History of Its Administration under Its Charters,* by Henry George Lyons (1944; reprint, Greenwood, 1968); and *Scientists and Amateurs: A History of the Royal Society,* by Dorothy Stimson (Greenwood, 1968).

On the Scientific Revolution more generally, see *The Scientific Revolution and the Origins of Modern Science,* by John Henry (St. Martin's, 1997); *Ingenious Pursuits: Building the Scientific Revolution,* by Lisa Jardine (Nan A. Talese, 1999); *It Started with Copernicus: How Turning the World Inside Out Led to the Scientific Revolution,* by Howard Margolis (McGraw-Hill, 2002); *The Scientific Revolution,* by Harry Henderson (Lucent, 1996); and *Isaac Newton and the Scientific Revolution,* by Gale E. Christianson (Oxford University Press, 1996).

For reference, see *Encyclopedia of the Scientific Revolution: From Copernicus to Newton,* edited by Wilbur Applebaum (Garland, 2000), and *The Scientific Revolution: An Encyclopedia,* by William E. Burns (ABC-CLIO, 2001).

55. Protestants Run for Cover

" **LOUIS XIV, REVOCATION OF THE EDICT OF NANTES, 1685**

See chapter 8 of
*An Age of Science
and Revolutions*

*In 1598, King Henry IV of France agreed to allow French Protestants,
called Huguenots, to worship as they wished in certain designated
places, as one way to end the civil wars over religion in France. The
decree, or official order, that guaranteed toleration was called the Edict
of Nantes, after the city in northwestern France where it was issued.
Catholics disliked the official policy of toleration because it allowed
Protestant churches to exist in the French kingdom—a kingdom that in
their opinion should be made up exclusively of Catholics. Almost a century later, in 1685, King Louis XIV—also called the Sun King because
he believed his court was the center of the universe, just like the sun—
finally revoked or ended this tolerant legislation with another decree
that banned Protestantism in his country. This made the French
Huguenots outlaws and sent them fleeing to other parts of the world,
including the Netherlands, Prussia (part of modern Germany), and
North America, to which they brought a wide range of crafts and
trades. Reform-minded and scientific thinkers of the Enlightenment saw
the suffering caused by the Revocation of the Edict of Nantes as evidence of Europeans' need to become more rational and tolerant.*

perpetual and >
irrevocable, never-
ending and
unchangeable

Be it known that . . . we have, by this present **perpetual and irrevocable** edict, suppressed and revoked, and do suppress and revoke,
the edict of our said grandfather, given at Nantes in April, 1598, in
its whole extent. . . .

R.P.R., initials that >
stood for Pretended
Reformed Religion,
another term for
Protestants; pretext,
supposed reason; fiefs,
territories

We forbid our subjects of the **R.P.R.** to meet any more for the
exercise of the said religion in any place or private house, under any
pretext whatever. . . .

We likewise forbid all noblemen, of what condition soever, to
hold such religious exercises in their houses or **fiefs**, under penalty
to be inflicted upon all our said subjects who shall engage in the
said exercises, of imprisonment and confiscation.

enjoin command >

We **enjoin** all ministers of the said R.P.R., who do not choose to
become converts and to embrace the Catholic . . . religion, to leave

fortnight, two weeks >

our kingdom and the territories subject to us within a **fortnight** of
the publication of our present edict. . . .

We forbid private schools for the instruction of children of the said R.P.R., and in general all things whatever which can be regarded as a concession of any kind in favor of the said religion.

As for children who may be born of persons of the said R.P.R., we desire that from henceforth they be baptized by the parish priests. We enjoin parents to send them to the churches for that purpose, under penalty of five hundred **livres** fine.

< **livres**, French money; 500 livres was a very large amount

The French Wars of Religion: Selected Documents, edited and translated by David Potter (St. Martin's, 1997), reprints a variety of texts related to the Edict of Nantes and issues of religious conflict in France. There are several accessible histories of the Reformation: *The Reformation*, by Owen Chadwick (Penguin, 1990); *The Reformation*, by Diarmaid MacCulloch (Viking, 2004); and *The World of the Reformation*, by Hans J. Hillerbrand (Scribner, 1973). *The Reformation: A Narrative History Related by Contemporary Observers and Participants*, also by Hillerbrand (Harper & Row, 1964), draws on many primary sources. *Protestantism*, by Stephen F. Brown (Facts on File, 2002), takes the history of Protestant churches from the Reformation to the present day.

56. Hitting the Books

SOR JUANA INÉS DE LA CRUZ, "REPLY TO SISTER PHILOTHEA," 1691

Sor (Sister) Juana Inés de la Cruz was a 17th-century Mexican nun who, besides praying and attending to her religious duties, loved to study and read all kinds of books. In the early modern era, monasteries of many religions around the world were often places where manuscripts and books were stored. They were also places where monks and nuns sometimes devoted themselves to writing philosophy, music, and poetry. As Roman Catholicism spread in colonial Mexico, monasteries and convents attracted devout people such as Sor Juana. She also entered the convent because she did not think that marriage was for her. Gradually her reputation for learning spread, as she began to write essays and compose poetry. But it angered some church officials that a woman would be so well read in different subjects such as philosophy and theology and accomplish so much as a writer. One official in particular published a letter that criticized her. He disguised the fact that a man was the author of the attack by signing it "Sister Philothea." In 1691, Sor Juana defended herself in the widely

See chapter 9 of *An Age of Science and Revolutions*

circulated letter below, pretending that she thought a woman had objected to her studies. Despite this defense, she gradually stopped her reading and writing and died a few years later. Her letter was published in 1700, after her death.

proposition, >
statement

I am ignorant and shudder to think that I might utter some disreputable **proposition** or distort the proper understanding of some passage or other [of the Bible]. My purpose in studying is not to write, much less to teach (this would be overbearing pride in my case), but simply to see whether studying makes me less ignorant. . . .

frivolities, less >
serious parts

curtail, cut short >

I became a nun because . . . given my total disinclination to marriage, it was the least unreasonable and most becoming choice I could make to assure my ardently desired salvation. To which consideration, as most important, all the other small **frivolities** of my nature yielded and gave way, such as my wish to live alone, to have no fixed occupation which might **curtail** my freedom to study, nor the noise of a community [of nuns] to interfere with the tranquil stillness of my books.

sound, correct, proper >

. . . Still I happily put up with all those drawbacks, for the sheer love of learning. Oh, if it had only been for the love of God, which would have been the **sound** way, what merit would have been mine! I *will* say that I tried to uplift my study as much as I could and direct it to serving Him, since the goal I aspired to was the study of theology. . . .

Why, for the ability . . . to compose verse, even when it was sacred verse, what nastiness have I not been subjected to, what unpleasantness has not come my way! I must say, Madam, that sometimes I stop and reflect that anyone who stands out—or whom God singles out, for He alone can do so—is viewed as everyone's

usurping, seizing, >
wrongfully taking
away; **coveted**,
greatly desired

enemy, because it seems to some that he is **usurping** the applause due them or deflecting the admiration which they have **coveted**, for which reason they pursue him.

A Sor Juana Anthology, translated by Alan S. Trueblood, with a foreword by Octavio Paz (Harvard University Press, 1988), provides an excellent selection of this Mexican writer's works. *The Answer: Including a Selection of Poems,* edited and translated by Electa Arenal and Amanda

Powell (Feminist Press at the City University of New York, 1994), and *The House of Trials*, translated by David Pasto (Peter Lang, 1996) are English versions of other works by Sor Juana. Selections by Sor Juana are included in *Treasury of Mexican Love Poems, Quotations, and Proverbs: In Spanish and English*, edited and translated by Enriqueta Carrington (Hippocrene, 2003), and *Six Masters of the Spanish Sonnet: Essays and Translations*, by Willis Barnstone (Southern Illinois University Press, 1993).

Sor Juana Inés de la Cruz is a biography for students by Gerard Flynn (Twayne, 1971). A more recent biography is *Sor Juana: Beauty and Justice in the Americas*, by Michelle A. Gonzalez (Orbis, 2003). There are chapters on Sor Juana in *The Church and Women in the Third World*, edited by John C. B. and Ellen Low Webster (Westminster Press, 1985); *Notable Latin American Women: Twenty-nine Leaders, Rebels, Poets, Battlers, and Spies, 1500-1900*, by Jerome R. Adams (McFarland, 1995), and, for younger students, *Mexican Portraits*, by Dorothy and Thomas Hoobler (Raintree Steck-Vaughn, 1993).

57. Coffee Break

ANTOINE GALLAND, ON THE ORIGIN AND DEVELOPMENT OF COFFEE, 1699

As Europeans launched their drive to explore the world and everything in it in the late 15th century, they also started enjoying many of the products used in other lands. Chocolate, tea, and coffee were just a few of these increasingly popular products. But they had to learn what to do with these new treasures. The Japanese and Chinese, for example, drank tea using especially beautiful cups, which the Europeans eventually figured out how to make. As a result, we still use the word "china" for the fine ceramic dishes that are now commonly used. People in the Ottoman Empire also drank coffee in a certain way—in coffeehouses, or what we also call cafés.

The French traveler and scholar Antoine Galland is best known for translating the Arabic tales of the Thousand and One Nights, *and for bringing to European attention characters from those stories, such as Sinbad the sailor and Aladdin and his magic lamp. He also wrote a popular little book about coffee in 1699. In it he explained to the French the Ottoman-Turks' methods of preparing coffee and their practice of drinking it in public gathering-places. Soon coffeehouses dotted European cities.*

See chapter 3 of
An Age of Science and Revolutions

These establishments which the Turks called in their language *Cahveh Khanch*—coffee houses—were at first frequented by studious people, those who went to pass a few hours with their friends and who formed in the cafés groups of twenty or thirty people who entertained one another while having a cup of coffee. When the conversation slowed down, some read from a book or, because in those days one found a number of poets in the houses, someone would recite a new poem that was then either praised or heatedly criticized. Others played checkers or backgammon. . . .

These groups passed unnoticed at the beginning but gradually became better known and the novelty, curiosity, and idleness slowly attracted young people finishing their studies and about to enter the legal profession, the out-of-work **Cadis** who were in Constantinople to seek reassignment to their post or to find a new job; the Muderis or professors who came to relax; and other sorts of people who, living from their investments, found more pleasure in this company than in remaining alone at home with nothing to do. Eventually, the coffee houses had such a high reputation that one would find there not only government officials of lower rank but even **Pashas** and the leading nobles of the **Sultan's** court, and it was at this time that there grew to be many coffee houses in various neighborhoods of this great city.

Cadis, Muslim> judges

Pashas, high-ranking> Turkish officers; **Sultan**, ruler of the Ottoman Empire

On the history of coffee, see *Tea and Coffee: A Modern View of Three Hundred Years of Tradition,* by Edward Bramah (Hutchinson, 1972), and *Uncommon Grounds: The History of Coffee and How It Transformed Our World,* by Mark Pendergrast (Basic, 1999).

The Book of Coffee, by Alain Stella (Flammarion, 1997), provides anecdotes about well-known coffee-lovers, and explains the importance of coffee in society beginning with the London coffeehouses of the 17th century. *Dr. Johnson's London: Coffee-houses and Climbing Boys, Medicine, Toothpaste, and Gin, Poverty and Press-gangs, Freakshows and Female Education,* by Liza Picard (St. Martin's, 2001), is an accessible, illustrated history of coffee drinking and other aspects of daily life in the English capital. *Coffee and Coffeehouses: The Origins of a Social Beverage in the Medieval Near East,* by Ralph S. Hattox (University of Washington Press, 1985), is a narrower scholarly study on the early history of coffee.

58. Out of Africa

PHILLIS WHEATLEY, "ON BEING BROUGHT FROM AFRICA TO AMERICA," 1770s

As a small child, Phillis Wheatley had seen more of the world than most of us today. She was born in Senegal in West Africa and then captured and sold into slavery, bound for the North American colonies. In 1761, the Massachusetts merchant John Wheatley and his wife, Susannah, bought the young African girl to be Mrs. Wheatley's personal servant. Their daughter taught Phillis to read, and she learned Latin and many other subjects. She soon began to write poetry. Although no American would publish a book of her verse, some of her poems were published in England, and Phillis Wheatley went to Britain to talk about her poetry. She wrote her poems in the grand style of her day, and readers in England admired her work for its ornate language. In her poems, she praised freedom and its defenders, such as George Washington, and described what it was like to be taken from one continent and sent to another as a slave. Despite the obstacles she faced, Phillis Wheatley's poetry has endured, and she is now a widely read poet.

See chapters 9 and 10 of *An Age of Science and Revolutions*

'Twas mercy brought me from my *Pagan* land,
Taught my **benighted** soul to understand   <benighted, ignorant
That there's a God, that there's a *Saviour* too:
Once I redemption neither sought nor knew.
Some view our **sable** race with scornful eye,   <sable, black
"Their colour is a **diabolic die**."   <diabolic die devilish dye, or color
Remember, *Christians*, Negros, black as *Cain*,
May be refin'd, and join **th'angelic train**.   <th'angelic train, the followers or admirers of Christ

Wheatley's poetry, letters, and various other writings have been collected in *The Collected Works of Phillis Wheatley*, edited by John C. Shields (Oxford University Press, 1988). A similar volume is *Wheatley's Complete Writings*, edited by Vincent Carretta (Penguin, 2001).

Phillis Wheatley , by Merle Richmond (Chelsea House, 1988), and *Phillis Wheatley: Legendary African-American Poet*, by Cynthia Salisbury (Enslow, 2001), are two biographies for young adults. *The Trials of Phillis Wheatley : America's First Black Poet and Her Encounters with the Founding Fathers*, by Henry Louis Gates (Basic Civitas, 2003), analyzes how

Founding Fathers such as Thomas Jefferson and George Washington and also African Americans themselves received Wheatley's poems. *Phillis Wheatley and Her Writings,* by William Henry Robinson (Garland, 1984), is a scholarly biography. Robinson's *Phillis Wheatley, a Bio-bibliography* (G.K. Hall, 1981) is a useful guide to further research.

59. Use Your Brain

66 | **IMMANUEL KANT, "ANSWER TO THE QUESTION: WHAT IS ENLIGHTENMENT?" 1784**

See introduction and chapter 8 of *An Age of Science and Revolutions*

Immanuel Kant was a German professor and one of the greatest philosophers of modern times. During the Enlightenment, a time when thinkers emphasized using reason and logic to solve problems, Kant led the way in promoting this cause. Instead of taking religious principles as the guide to behavior, he tried to find rational grounds for behaving well so that people could make their own decisions about morality—that is, doing the right thing. In 1784 a Berlin society offered a prize for defining what this new trend toward reason was, and Kant responded with this essay, which originally appeared in a Berlin journal and was then published in his collected works. It has influenced people down to our own times because it gives a clear definition of the Enlightenment.

Enlightenment is man's emergence from his self-imposed nonage. Nonage is the inability to use one's own understanding without another's guidance. This nonage is self-imposed if its cause lies not in lack of understanding but in indecision and lack of courage to use one's own mind without another's guidance. Dare to know! ... "Have the courage to use your own understanding," is therefore the motto of the Enlightenment.

Laziness and cowardice are the reasons why such a large part of mankind gladly remain **minors** all their lives, long after nature has freed them from external guidance. They are the reasons why it is so easy for others to set themselves up as guardians. It is so comfortable to be a minor. If I have a book that thinks for me, a pastor who acts as my conscience, a physician who prescribes my diet, and

minors, people not> legally responsible for themselves, such as children so on—then I have no need to exert myself. I have no need to think, if only I can pay; others will take care of the disagreeable business for me. . . .

Thus it is very difficult for the individual to work himself out of the nonage which has become almost second nature to him. He has even grown to like it, and is at first really incapable of using his own understanding because he has never been permitted to try it. **Dogmas** and formulas, these mechanical tools designed for reasonable use—or rather abuse—of his natural gifts, are the **fetters** of an everlasting nonage. The man who casts them off would make an uncertain leap over the narrowest ditch, because he is not used to such free movement. That is why there are only a few men who walk firmly, and who have emerged from nonage by **cultivating** their own minds. . . .

< **dogma**, a set of principles, especially religious principles; **fetter**, a metal loop around the ankle used to restrain prisoners; **cultivating**, improving

Enlightenment requires nothing but *freedom*—and the most innocent of all that may be called "freedom": freedom to make public use of one's reason in all matters. Now I hear the cry from all sides: "Do not argue!" The officer says: "Do not argue—**drill**!" The tax collector: "Do not argue—pay!" The pastor: "Do not argue—believe!" . . . We find restrictions on freedom everywhere. But which restriction is harmful to enlightenment? I reply: the public use of one's reason must be free at all times, and this alone can bring enlightenment to mankind.

< **drill**, do military exercises

An Immanuel Kant Reader, edited and translated by Blakney, Raymond Bernard Blakney (Harper, 1960), provides a good selection of Kant's works. *Kant in 90 Minutes,* by Paul Strathern (Ivan R. Dee, 1996), *On Kant,* by Grant Thomson (Wadsworth/Thomson Learning, 2000), and *Kant: A Very Short Introduction,* by Roger Scruton (Oxford University Press, 2001), are good introductions to the philosopher's work. *The Cambridge Companion to Kant,* edited by Paul Guyer (Cambridge University Press, 1992), and *A Kant Dictionary,* by Howard Caygill (Blackwell, 1995), are useful references.

60. Japan Meets the Scientific Revolution

" SUGITA GEMPAKU, "A DUTCH ANATOMY LESSON IN JAPAN," 1771

See chapters 6 and 7
of *An Age of Science
and Revolutions*

Many people believe that Japan closed itself off to the rest of the world in the early modern period because the Japanese people thought that traders, missionaries, and other strangers threatened their traditional way of life. But the Japanese did have contact with foreigners in the 18th century, and curious Japanese people kept track of what was going on with them—especially with those who came from Europe. Early modern Japanese people also looked at foreign art, read foreign books, and discussed foreign ideas. In 1771 a Japanese doctor, Sugita Gempaku, got hold of a Dutch medical book, and the contents of the book drastically changed his ideas about medicine. He wrote about his reaction to the Dutch book in his memoir. This sharing of ideas made him part of the Enlightenment that was circling the globe. Ideas from around the world helped to develop Japan's interest in trade, and these ideas inspired some of Japan's nobles to lead a revolution in the 19th century to make Japan more scientific and industrial.

happening, event >

Commissioner,
official;
post-mortem, after
death; condemned,
sentenced to death >

Ryotaku, a friend
of the author >

kimono, long robe >

anatomy, study of the >
human body; *Tabulae
Anatomicae* Latin for
"anatomical tables";
Nagasakin, Nagasaki,
port city

dissection, cutting >
open for study, in early
modern times often
done by a butcher

It was a strange and even miraculous **happening** that I was able to obtain that book in that particular spring of 1771. Then at the night of the third day of the third month, I received a letter from a man by the name of Tokuno, who was in the service of the Town **Commissioner.** Tokuno stated in his letter that "A **post-mortem examination** of the body of a **condemned** criminal by a resident physician will be held tomorrow. . . . You are welcome to witness it if you so desire."

The next day, when we arrived at the location . . . **Ryotaku** reached under his **kimono** to produce a Dutch book and showed it to us. "This is a Dutch book of **anatomy** called *Tabulae Anatomicae.* I bought this a few years ago when I went to **Nagasakin,** and kept it." As I examined it, it was the same book I had and was of the same edition. . . .

Thereafter we went together to the place which was especially set for us to observe the **dissection.** . . . That day, the old **butcher** pointed to this and that organ. After the heart, liver, gall bladder, and stomach were identified, he pointed to other parts for which there were no names. "I don't know their names. But I have dissected quite a few bodies from my youthful days. Inside of everyone's abdomen there were these parts and those parts." The old butcher again said, "Every time I had a dissection, I pointed out to those physicians many of these parts, but not a single one of them questioned 'What was this?' or 'What was that?'" We compared the body as dissected against the charts both Ryotaku and I had, and could not find a single **variance** from the charts. The *Chinese Book of Medicine* says that the lungs are like the eight petals of the **lotus flower,** with three petals hanging in front, three in back, and two petals forming like two ears and that the liver has three petals to the left and four petals to the right. There were no such divisions, and the positions and shapes of intestines and **gastric** organs were all different from those taught by the old theories. . . .

< **variance,** change, or difference; **lotus flower,** water lily, also a Buddhist religious symbol

< **gastric,** relating to the stomach

On the way home we spoke to each other and felt the same way. "How marvelous was our actual experience today. It is a shame that we were ignorant of these things until now. . . . How disgraceful it is. Somehow through this experience, let us investigate further the truth about the human body. If we practice medicine with this knowledge behind us, we can make contributions for people under heaven and on this earth."

The Making of Modern Japan, by Marius B. Jansen (Harvard University Press, 2000), is particularly strong on Japan's interactions with the West. See also *The Modern History of Japan: From Tokugawa Times to the Present,* by Andrew Gordon (Oxford University Press, 2003). *Japan Meets the World: Japan from Shogun to Sony, 1543–1984,* by John R. Roberson, (Milbrook, 1998) is a good history for young adults.

61. Citizens!

See chapter 10 of
*An Age of Science
and Revolutions*

*The French Revolution, which broke out in Paris in 1789, was full of
demonstrations, crowd scenes, and violence. Besides being a time of
fighting and bloodshed, it was also a time when the French thought
seriously about how to change society and politics. Having decided
that they were no longer the subjects of a king but independent and
self-governing citizens, the revolutionaries thought a great deal about
what their new status meant. At this time, using ideas from the
Enlightenment, people in many parts of the world, including the
British colonies of North America, focused on how to protect citizens
from abuse by kings, the military, and other powers. During the summer of 1789, the National Assembly of France, a new institution composed of representatives of the people, drew up a declaration about the
basic rights of citizens. Soon after, the government of the new United
States added a Bill of Rights to the U.S. Constitution, which shares
some of the themes of the French Declaration of the Rights of Man.*

The representatives of the French people, organized as a National
Assembly, believing that the ignorance, neglect, or contempt of the
rights of man are the sole cause of public **calamities** and of the corruption of governments, have determined to set forth in a solemn
declaration of the natural, **inalienable**, and sacred rights of man, in
order that this declaration, being constantly before all the members
of **the social body**, shall remind them continually of their rights and
duties; in order that the acts of the legislative power, as well as those
of the executive power, may be compared at any moment with the
objects and purposes of all political institutions. . . . Therefore the
National Assembly recognizes and proclaims, in the presence and
under the **auspices of the Supreme Being**, the following rights of
man and of the citizen:

> **calamities,** disasters

> **inalienable,** unable to
be taken away

> **the social body,**
society

**auspices of the
Supreme Being,**
authority of God;
general good, that is,
differences between
groups of people can
only be recognized
if they benefit
> everybody

Article 1. Men are born and remain free and equal in rights.
Social distinctions may be found only upon the **general good**.

Article 2. The aim of all political association is the preservation of the natural and **imprescriptible rights** of man. These rights are liberty, property, security, and resistance to oppression.

> < **imprescriptible rights,** rights that cannot be forbidden; **sovereignty,** greatest power

Article 3. The principle of all **sovereignty** resides essentially in the nation. No body nor individual may exercise any authority which does not proceed directly from the nation. . . .

Article 9. As all persons are held innocent until they shall have been declared guilty, if arrest shall be deemed **indispensable**, all harshness not essential to the securing of the prisoner's person shall be severely repressed by law.

> < **indispensable,** absolutely necessary

Article 10. No one shall be **disquieted** on account of his opinions, including his religious views, provided their manifestation does not disturb the public order established by law.

> < **disquieted,** bothered

Article 11. The free communication of ideas and opinions is one of the most precious of the rights of man. Every citizen may, accordingly, speak, write, and print with freedom. . . .

📖 *The French Revolution and Human Rights: A Brief Documentary History,* by Lynn Hunt (Bedford/St. Martin's, 1996), and *The Enlightenment: A Brief History with Documents,* by Margaret C. Jacob (Bedford/St. Martin's, 2001), provide a useful selection of related documents. Other excellent anthologies include *The Age of Enlightenment: The 18th-century Philosophers,* edited by Isaiah Berlin (New American Library, 1984); *The Enlightenment: A Sourcebook and Reader,* edited by Paul Hyland and others (Routledge, 2003); *The Enlightenment: A Comprehensive Anthology,* by Peter Gay (Simon and Schuster, 1973), and *The Portable Enlightenment Reader,* edited by Isaac Kramnick (Penguin, 1995).

Age of Enlightenment, by Peter Gay (Time-Life Books, 1966), is a well-illustrated history for the general reader. A general history for young adults is *The Enlightenment,* by John M. Dunn (Lucent, 1999).

62. Battle Cry of Freedom

❝ TOUSSAINT L'OUVERTURE, PROCLAMATION OF A SLAVE REVOLUTION IN THE CARIBBEAN, 1793

Pierre Dominique Toussaint L'Ouverture, a literate slave and one of the leaders of a successful 1791 slave uprising on the French island colony of Saint-Domingue (present-day Haiti), was inspired by the

> See chapter 10 of *An Age of Science and Revolutions*

ideals of the French Revolution. Many white and a few black slave-holders ran sugar plantations on the island, treating their workers brutally, and the concepts of freedom, equality, and brotherhood of all peoples quickly captured the imagination of the enslaved people of Saint-Domingue. In this proclamation, Toussaint L'Ouverture uses the language of the European Enlightenment to express the goals of a slave revolt on the other side of the Atlantic.

Brothers and friends, I am Toussaint L'Ouverture, my name is perhaps known to you. I have undertaken vengeance. I want Liberty and Equality to reign in **San Domingo.** I work to bring them into existence. Unite yourselves to us, brothers, and fight with us for the same cause, etc.

San Domingo, > from the Spanish name for their half of the island, Santo Domingo

Your very humble and very obedient servant

Toussaint L'Ouverture
General of the **Armies of the King, for the Public Good**

King, because the > date of the proclamation is not known, Toussaint L'Ouverture could either be referring to Louis XVI or XVII of France. Although he sympathized with the goals of the Revolution, Toussaint L'Ouverture was loyal to the king, as were many revolutionaries.

Toussaint L'Ouverture: The Fight for Haiti's Freedom, by Walter Dean Myers (Simon & Schuster, 1996), is written for children but reproduces the series of paintings on the subject by the distinguished African-American artist Jacob Lawrence. *Toussaint L'Ouverture,* by Thomas and Dorothy Hoobler (Chelsea House, 1990), is a solid biography for young adults. *"This Gilded African": Toussaint L'Ouverture,* by Wanda Parkinson (Quartet Books/Horizon, 1978), is another biography. *Avengers of the New World: The Story of the Haitian Revolution,* by Laurent Dubois (Harvard University Press, 2004), is a recent scholarly study of that landmark event.

TIMELINE

300
Franks and other Germanic peoples settle on the Rhine River, in present-day Germany

300–400
Founding of Ghana, one of the earliest kingdoms of western Sudan; gold is mined at Bambuk, in Africa; Jenne, in Africa, becomes an important market city

303
Roman emperor Diocletian issues order persecuting Christians

313
Roman emperor Constantine converts to Christianity and grants toleration to Christians

330
Constantine moves the capital of the Roman Empire to Constantinople, in present-day Turkey

360
Huns invade Europe

401
Visigoths, under leadership of Alaric, invade Italy

410
Visigoths sack Rome; Roman legions withdraw from England

420
St. Augustine writes *The City of God*

433–53
Attila leads the Huns in attacks on Europe

450
Saxons, Angles, and Jutes invade Britain

476
Western Roman Empire comes to an end

510
Clovis, king of the Franks, converts to Christianity

527–65
Justinian I, the Great, and his wife, Theodora, rule the Byzantine Empire, make their body of laws and legal principles, build the church Hagia Sophia, and finance military campaigns to regain the Western Empire

529
St. Benedict founds a monastery at Mount Cassino, Italy

542
Outbreak of bubonic plague in western Europe and the Byzantine Empire

596
Pope Gregory I, the Great, sends missionaries to England

604
Prince Shotoku issues the 17-Article Constitution in Japan

610–32
Muhammad hears the word of God and recounts it to his followers; Islam is born

about 610–47
King Harsha reigns in India

618
Li Yuan founds the Tang dynasty in China

622
Muhammad moves to Medina (the Hegira), marking the start of the Islamic calendar

624
Muhammad's followers defeat Meccans; Arabs unify under Islam

629–42
Chinese monk Xuanzang travels to India

632
Arabs expand their territory into the Byzantine Empire

632–47
Queen Sondok rules the kingdom of Silla, Korea

634
Election of the second caliph (Islamic ruler), Umar

643–711
Arabs take possession of North Africa

646
Taika reforms introduce Chinese-style government to Japan

653
Third caliph, Uthman, orders that the Quran be written down

656
Fourth caliph, Ali, assumes power

661–750
Umayyad caliphs reign in Damascus, in present-day Syria

668
Kingdom of Silla unifies Korea

680
An army sent by the Umayyad caliph ambushes and murders Husayn at Karbala, Iraq

690–705
Reign of Wu Zhao, female emperor of China

700–900
Muslim traders arrive in western and central Sudan

710
Japanese court moves to a newly built capital at Nara

711
Muslims invade and occupy Spain

732
Charles Martel stops Arabs from expanding their territory in western Europe at the Battle of Tours and Poitiers

747–52
Great Buddha statue is built at Nara, Japan

762–63
Caliph al-Mansur founds Baghdad, capital city of the great Abbasid caliphs

768
Charles the Great becomes king of the Franks

787
Vikings begin attacks on England

790
Golden period of Arabic learning begins in Baghdad during the reign of Harun al-Rashid

about 800
Buddhist temple-mountain is built at Borobudur, Java

800
Pope Leo III crowns Charlemagne emperor

800–1000
Sudanese begin to convert to Islam

840
Norwegians attack Ireland and found Dublin

843
Treaty of Verdun divides the Carolingian Empire into three parts

862
Rus state is established at Novgorod

900
Feudalism begins to develop in Europe

907
End of the Tang dynasty in China

918
Wang Kon founds the Koryo dynasty, and reunifies Korea

960
Zhao Kuangyin founds the Song dynasty in China

962
Otto the Great revives the Holy Roman Empire and is crowned emperor by the pope

969
Fatamid caliphate is established in Egypt; city of Cairo is founded

988
Vladimir of Kiev, Russia (present-day Ukraine), marries a Byzantine princess and converts to Christianity

997–1027
Fujiwara Michinaga is the power behind the throne in Heian Japan

about 1000
Norwegian Vikings reach the North American coast

1000–1300
Africans mine gold at Mapungubwe, a kingdom in what is now northern South Africa

about 1010
Murasaki Shikibu writes *The Tale of Genji*

1020
Venice, Genoa, and Pisa emerge as powerful cities in Italy

1025
Romanesque architecture reaches its height in Europe

1054
Great Schism occurs between Rome and Constantinople

1055
Seljuk Turks establish a sultanate in Baghdad

1066
William of Normandy invades England and becomes king

1071
Seljuk Turks win the Battle of Manzikert and invade Anatolia

about 1076
Almoravids invade Ghana

1076
Pope Gregory VII excommunicates Henry IV of Germany

1077
Henry IV travels to Canossa in the Alps to seek the pope's forgiveness

about 1090s to early 1100s
al-Ghazali persuades the Ulema to accept Sufism

1091
Normans conquer Sicily

1095
Pope Urban II calls for the First Crusade

1099
Crusaders take Jerusalem and establish the Latin Kingdom of Jerusalem

about 1100
Omar Khayyam writes his *Rubiyyat*

1100–1500
Yoruba kingdom of Ifé flourishes in West Africa's rain forest

1115
Jurchen Jin dynasty is founded in northern China; St. Bernard founds Clairvaux

1119
University of Bologna is established in present-day Italy

1120
Scholastic philosophy and troubadour poetry and music develop in Europe

1122
Concordat of Worms settles whether the king or pope has more authority in what is known as the Investiture Controversy

1127
Song dynasty loses northern China, moves capital to Hangzhou (present day Lin'an)

1142
Peter Abelard, scholastic philosopher, dies

1150
University of Paris is established in France

1167
The pope crowns Frederick I Holy Roman Emperor

1170
Knights of Henry II, king of England, murder Thomas à Becket, archbishop of Canterbury

1192–98
Innocent III is pope, marking the height of the medieval papacy

1200–1400
African kingdom of Great Zimbabwe is the center of a commercial empire that provides gold to coastal Swahili traders

1206
Qutb-ud-Din Aybak founds the Delhi Sultanate in India; Genghis Khan becomes Mongol leader

1215
Nobles, townsmen, and knights defeat King John I of England at the Battle of Runnymede and signs the Magna Carta

1220
Mongols take over the Silk Road cities of Bukhara and Samarkand

1223
Russians lose to Mongols at the Battle of Kalka, in present-day Ukraine or in eastern Europe

1228
Holy Roman Emperor Frederick II makes a treaty with Muslims on a crusade in the Holy Land

1235
Sundiata becomes the first king of the Mali Empire

1236
Raziya becomes the first and only woman sultan of Delhi

1258
Mongols destroy Baghdad; Osman establishes the Ottoman Empire

1264
Khubilai Khan makes a capital at Beijing and begins the Yuan dynasty

1265
Simon de Montfort calls the first Parliament in England

1270
Mongols establish effective rule in Korea

1273
Thomas Aquinas writes *Summa Theologica*

1274
Japanese defeat the first Mongol invasion

1279
End of the Song dynasty in China; Khubilai Khan's Yuan dynasty controls all of China

1292
Marco Polo returns to Italy from China

1300
Kingdom of Benin is founded in the rain forest of West Africa, in present-day Nigeria

1302
Philip IV, the Fair, convenes the first Estates General in France at which all three estates (nobility, clergy, and commoners) are represented

1305
Clement V becomes pope and moves the papacy to Avignon, France

1313
Civil service examinations are reinstated in China under Mongol rule

1324–25
Mansa Musa of Mali makes his pilgrimage to Mecca

1325
Zen influence grows in Japan

1325–54
Ibn Battuta travels around the world

1326
Brothers Harihara and Bukka Sangama
found the kingdom of Vijayanagara in
southern India

1337
Dante completes *The Divine Comedy*

1337–1453
Hundred Years' War is waged in Europe

1338
Plague spreads rapidly into the Near East,
Europe, and North Africa

1368
Taizu founds the Ming dynasty in China

1380
Russians defeat the Golden Horde at
Kulikovo

1380s–1405
Tamerlane rules Central and South Asia

1386
Jogaila and Jadwiga marry and unite
Poland and Lithuania

1387
Ottomans defeat Serbs at Kossovo;
Geoffrey Chaucer begins to write his
Canterbury Tales

1400–50
Great Zimbabwe is abandoned and the
kingdom of Mwenemutapa is founded in
Africa

1400–1591
Mali is in decline; Songhay begins expansion in Africa

1400–1800
Oyo, a forest kingdom of Yoruba, thrives

1405–1433
Chinese admiral Zheng He commands
voyages to the Indian Ocean

1410
Poles and Lithuanians defeat Teutonic
Knights at Tannenberg in northeastern
Europe

1415
Czech clergyman Jan Hus is burned as a
heretic for his writings on religious reform

1419–50
King Sejong rules the Choson dynasty
during Korea's "golden age"

1431
Joan of Arc is burned at Rouen, France

1441
First shipment of African slaves to
Portugal

1450s
Johannes Gutenberg invents a printing
press in Europe

1450–1500
First Muslims arrive at Mwenemutapa

1451–81
Sultan Mehmed II rules the Ottoman
Empire

1453
Ottomans defeat Byzantines and take over
Constantinople

1485
Henry Tudor defeats Richard III at the
Battle of Bosworth Field and starts the
Tudor line as Henry VI

1492
Columbus makes his first voyage to the Americas; kingdom of Granada falls; Isabella and Ferdinand push the Jews out of Spain

1493–1528
Askia the Great rules the Songhay Empire in Africa

1494
Pope makes the Treaty of Tordesillas, dividing the world between Spain and Portugal

1497–99
Vasco da Gama sails around Africa and reaches India

1502
First African slaves are brought to the Americas

1503–5
Portuguese sack and then destroy Kilwa on the coast of East Africa

1503
Leonardo da Vinci paints *Mona Lisa*

1510s
Guru Nanak Devi Ji, founder of Sikhism, begins teaching in India

1513
Niccolò Machiavelli writes *The Prince*

1515
First sugar mill in the Western Hemisphere is built

1519–21
Ferdinando Magellan leads a voyage around the world

1520s
Protestant Reformation begins

1520–66
Suleiman "the Magnificent" rules the Ottoman Empire

1521
Hernán Cortés conquers the Aztec Empire

1526
Babur takes over northern India at the Battle of Panipat; Turks win a battle at Mohacs in eastern Europe to extend their territorial control

1533
Francisco Pizarro conquers the Inca Empire

1540
Ignatius Loyola establishes the Jesuits

1540s
Europeans find that Peru is rich in silver

1543
Publication of Nicolaus Copernicus's *The Revolutions of the Heavenly Spheres*, announcing the sun-centered universe

1555–1603
Queen Elizabeth I rules England

1556–98
King Philip II rules Spain

1556–1605
Mughal emperor Akbar the Great rules India

1588
England defeats the Spanish Armada

1595
First compound microscope is invented

1596
Shakespeare's *Romeo and Juliet* is probably first performed

1598
Tang Xianzu finishes *The Peony Pavilion*

1600
Matteo Ricci sets up a Jesuit mission in China; East India Trading Company is founded

1605
Jahangir begins reign over Mughal India

1607
Colonists establish Jamestown, Virginia, the first permanent English settlement in North America

1609
Galileo invents his telescope; Johannes Kepler publishes his *New Astronomy*

1610
Jesuits and Chinese mathematicians face off over astronomical predictions

1616
British East India Company establishes an outpost in Mughal India

1619
First ship carrying African slaves arrives in Virginia

1620
Pilgrims land near Plymouth Rock in Massachusetts

1624
Dutch found a settlement on Manhattan island called New Amsterdam

1628
Shah Jahan begins to rule Mughal India; William Harvey publishes *Anatomical Exercise on the Motion of the Heart and Blood in Animals,* describing how the blood circulates from the heart

1631–47
Shah Jahan builds the Taj Mahal

1632–33
Galileo publishes *Dialogue Concerning the Two Chief World Systems,* defending the sun-centered view of the universe; he is condemned by the Inquisition and forced to renounce his belief in Copernicus's theory

1637
Descartes publishes *Discourse on Method,* which includes his statement "I think, therefore I am."

1644
Manchus bring the Ming dynasty to an end and the Qing Empire begins in China

1649
Charles I of England is beheaded for being a tyrant and enemy of the nation

1658
Aurangzeb becomes ruler of Mughal India

1661
Kangxi begins successful reign in China

1667
Peace treaty between the Dutch and English gives the American territory of "New Amsterdam" to the British

1676
Peter the Great, Ivan IV, and regent Sophia share power in Russia

1683
Turks invade Austria and are driven back by King Sobieski of Poland

1687
Newton publishes *Mathematical Principles of Natural Philosophy,* the basis of modern physics and astronomy

1689
John Locke publishes *Two Treatises of Government,* challenging the divine authority of kings and laying the foundation of modern democratic and constitutional government; William and Mary of Orange succeed James II in England during the Glorious Revolution, which produces the Bill of Rights

1699
English establish their first trading post in China

1717
Lady Mary Montagu publishes a letter in England on small pox inoculation in Turkey

1721
Montesquieu publishes the *Persian Letters,* containing a critique of European customs

1725
Peter the Great dies after instituting major reforms in Russia

1728
Jai Sing starts building observatories in India and builds the newly designed city of Jaipur

1740
Maria Theresa inherits the Habsburg throne

1743
Benjamin Franklin begins his experiments with electricity

1751
First volume of the French *Encyclopédie* published, challenging the authority of the Christian church and legitimacy of kings

1763
Treaty of Paris ends the French and Indian War between France and Britain in America

1771
First modern Turkish medical textbook is published

1776
American Revolution begins with publication of the Declaration of Independence; Adam Smith publishes *The Wealth of Nations*

1787
United States Constitution drafted

1789
French Revolution begins and the country adopts the Declaration of the Rights of Man and the Citizen

1791
Toussaint L'Ouverture leads a slave uprising in San Domingue, which leads to the establishment of the independent republic of Haiti

1792
Mary Wollstonecraft publishes *Vindication of the Rights of Women* in England

FURTHER READING

AFRICA AND THE MIDDLE EAST

McKissack, Patricia, and Frederick McKissack. *The Royal Kingdoms of Ghana, Mali, and Songhay: Life in Medieval Africa.* New York: Henry Holt, 1994.

McNeill, William, and Marilyn Waldman, eds. *The Islamic World.* New York: Oxford University Press, 1973.

Quigley, Mary. *Ancient West African Kingdoms: Ghana, Mali, and Songhai.* Chicago: Heinemann Library, 2002.

Wheatcroft, Andrew. *The Ottomans.* New York: Viking, 1993.

THE AMERICAS

Baquedano, Elizabeth. *Aztec, Inca, and Maya.* New York: Dorling Kindersley, 1993.

Berdan, Frances. *The Aztecs.* New York: Chelsea House, 1989.

Bullock, Steven C. *The American Revolution: A History in Documents.* New York: Oxford University Press, 2003

Lepore, Jill. *Encounters in the New World: A History in Documents.* New York: Oxford University Press, 2000.

Maestro, Betsy, and Giulio Maestro. *Exploration and Conquest: The Americas after Columbus 1500–1620.* New York: Mulberry, 1997.

Palmer, Colin. *The First Passage: Blacks in the Americas 1502–1617.* New York: Oxford University Press, 1995.

Wood, Tim. *The Incas.* New York: Viking, 1996.

ASIA

Bérinstain, Valerie. *India and the Mughal Dynasty.* New York: Abrams, 1998.

DuBois, Jill. *Korea.* 2nd ed. New York: Benchmark, 2005.

Hansen, Valerie. *The Open Empire: A History of China to 1600.* New York: W. W. Norton, 2000.

Major, John S. *The Land and People of Mongolia.* New York: Lippincott, 1990.

Morgan, David *The Mongols.* Oxford, England: Blackwell, 1990.

Nardo, Don. *Traditional Japan.* San Diego, Calif.: Lucent, 1995

Shelley, Rex, Teo Chuu Yong, and Russell Mok. *Japan.* 2nd ed. New York: Benchmark, 2002.

EUROPE AND RUSSIA

Almedingen, E. M. *Land of Muscovy: The History of Early Russia.* New York: Farrar, Straus & Giroux, 1972.

Corrick, James A. *The Byzantine Empire.* San Diego, Calif.: Lucent, 1997.

Dunn, John M. *The Enlightenment.* San Diego, Calif.: Lucent, 1999.

Hanawalt, Barbara A. *The Middle Ages: An Illustrated History.* New York: Oxford University Press, 1998.

ATLASES

Black, Jeremy. *DK Atlas of World History.* New York: Dorling Kindersley, 2000.

Haywood, John. *World Atlas of the Past.* 4 vols. New York: Oxford University Press, 1999.

McEvedy, Colin, and David Woodruff. *The New Penguin Atlas of Medieval History.* New York: Penguin, 1992.

O'Brien, Patrick K. *Atlas of World History.* New York: Oxford University Press, 1999.

Rand McNally Children's Atlas of World History. Chicago: Rand McNally, 1988.

DICTIONARIES AND ENCYCLOPEDIAS

Applebaum, Wilbur. *Encyclopedia of the Scientific Revolution: From Copernicus to Newton.* New York: Garland, 2000.

Bergin, Thomas G., and Jennifer Speake, eds. *Encyclopedia of the Renaissance and Reformation.* New York: Facts on File, 2004.

English, Edward. *Encyclopedia of the Medieval World.* New York: Facts on File, 2005.

Friedman, John Block, and Kristin Mossler Figg, eds. *Trade, Travel, and Exploration in the Middle Ages: An Encyclopedia.* New York: Garland, 2000.

Grendler, Paul F., and the Renaissance Society of America, eds. *Encylopedia of the Renaissance.* 6 vols. New York: Charles Scribner's Sons, 2000.

Jordan, William Chester, ed. *The Middle Ages: An Encyclopedia for Students.* New York: Charles Scribner's Sons, 1996.

Wilson, Katharina M., and Nadia Margolis. *Women in the Middle Ages: An Encyclopedia.* 2 vols. Westport, Conn.: Greenwood, 2004.

BIOGRAPHIES

Butson, Thomas G. *Ivan the Terrible.* New York: Chelsea House, 1987.

Calvert, Patricia. *Hernando Cortes: Fortune Favored the Bold.* New York: Benchmark, 2002.

Davis, A. R. *Tu Fu.* Boston: Twayne, 1971.

Davis, Thomas. *John Calvin.* New York: Chelsea House, 2004.

Dunn, Ross E. *The Adventures of Ibn Battuta: A Muslim Traveler of the Fourteenth Century.* Berkeley: University of California Press, 1986.

Flynn, Gerard. *Sor Juana Inés de la Cruz.* Boston: Twayne, 1971.

Freedman, Russell. *Confucius: The Golden Rule.* New York: Arthur A. Levine, 2002.

Hoobler, Thomas, and Dorothy Hoobler. *Toussaint L'Ouverture.* New York: Chelsea House, 1990.

Hynson, Colin. *Columbus and the Renaissance Explorers.* New York: Barron's, 2000.

Kent, Zachary. *Christopher Columbus.* Chicago: Children's Press, 1991.

Marty, Martin. *Martin Luther.* New York: Penguin, 2004.

Mee, Charles L., Jr. *Erasmus: The Eye of the Hurricane.* New York: Coward, McCann, and Geoghegan, 1974.

Meyer, Edith Patterson. *First Lady of the Renaissance: A Biography of Isabella d'Este.* Boston: Little, Brown, 1970.

Rawding, F. W. *The Buddha.* Minneapolis, Minn.: Lerner, 1979.

Salisbury, Cynthia. *Phillis Wheatley: Legendary African-American Poet.* Berkeley Heights, N.J.: Enslow, 2001.

Stanley, Diane. *Peter the Great.* New York: Morrow, 1999.

Stefoff, Rebecca. *Vasco da Gama and the Portuguese Explorers.* New York: Chelsea House, 1993.

Stepanek, Sally. *Martin Luther.* New York: Chelsea House, 1986.

Stevens, Paul. *Ferdinand and Isabella.* New York: Chelsea House, 1988.

Taylor, Ivan E. *Samuel Pepys.* Boston: Twayne, 1989.

Townsend, Camilla. *Pocahontas and the Powhatan Dilemma.* New York: Hill and Wang, 2004.

Wriggens, Sally Hovey. *Xuanzang: A Buddhist Pilgrim on the Silk Road.* Boulder, Colo.: Westview, 1996.

Zuffi, Stefano. *Dürer.* New York: DK, 1999.

ANTHOLOGIES AND READERS

Chang, Kang-i San, and Huan Saussy, eds. *Women Writers of Traditional China: An Anthology of Poetry and Criticism.* Stanford, Calif.: Stanford University Press, 1999.

De Bary, William Theodore, and Irene Bloom. *Sources of Chinese Tradition.* 2nd ed. New York: Columbia University Press, 1999.

[66] De Bary, William Theodore, et al. *Sources of Indian Tradition.* New York: Columbia University Press, 1988.

Freeman-Grenville, G. S. P., ed. and trans. *The East African Coast: Select Documents from the First to the Earlier Nineteenth Century.* London: Rex Collins, 1975.

[66] Graham, A. C. *Poems of the Late T'ang.* London: Penguin, 1965.

[66] Hopkins, J. F. P., and N. Levtzion. *Corpus of Early Arabic Sources for West African History.* New York: Cambridge University Press, 1981.

Kline, Daniel T. *Medieval Literature for Children.* New York: Routledge, 2003.

Kramnick, Isaac. *The Portable Enlightenment Reader.* New York: Penguin, 1995.

Latham, Robert, and William Matthews, eds. *A Pepys Anthology: Passages from the Diary of Samuel Pepys.* Berkeley: University of California Press, 1988.

[66] Lee, Peter, and William Theodore de Bary. *Sources of Korean Tradition: From Early Times through the Sixteenth Century.* New York: Columbia University Press, 1997–2000.

Naphy, William G., ed. *Documents on the Continental Reformation.* New York: St. Martin's, 1996.

[66] Ross, James Bruce, ed. *The Portable Renaissance Reader.* New York: Viking, 1968.

Ross, James Bruce, and Mary Martin McLaughlin. *The Medieval Reader.* New York: Penguin, 1977.

Seth, Vikram, trans. *Three Chinese Poets: Translations of Poems by Wang Wei, Li Bai, and Du Fu.* New York: HarperPerennial, 1993.

Shields, John C., ed. *The Collected Works of Phillis Wheatley.* New York: Oxford University Press, 1988.

[66] Tharu, Susie, and K. Lalita, eds. *Women Writing in India, 600 B.C. to the Present.* London: Pandora, 1991.

[66] Trueblood, Alan S., trans. *A Sor Juana Anthology.* Cambridge, Mass.: Harvard University Press, 1988.

[66] Tsunoda, Ryusaku, William Theodore de Bary, and Donald Keene. *Sources of Japanese Tradition.* 2nd edition. New York: Columbia University Press, 2001.

Wang, Robin, ed. *Images of Women in Chinese Thought and Culture: Writings from the Pre-Qin Period through the Song Dynasty.* Indianapolis: Hackett, 2003.

White, Barbara Sue. *Chinese Women: A Thousand Pieces of Gold, An Anthology.* New York: Oxford University Press, 2003.

ARTS AND CRAFTS

Barter, James. *A Renaissance Painter's Studio.* San Diego, Calif.: Lucent, 2002.

Benton, Janetta Rebold. *The Art of the Middle Ages.* London: Thames and Hudson, 2002.

Craven, Roy C. *Indian Art.* Revised ed. New York: Thames & Hudson, 1997.

Girard-Geslan, Maud, et al. *Art of Southeast Asia.* New York: Abrams, 1998.

Lassieur, Allison. *Leonardo da Vinci and the Renaissance in World History.* Berkeley Heights, N.J.: Enslow, 2000.

Mason, Antony. *In the Time of Michelangelo.* Brookfield, Conn.: Copper Beech, 2001.

Sekules, Veronica. *Medieval Art.* New York: Oxford University Press, 2001.

Stanley-Baker, Joan. *Japanese Art.* Revised ed. New York: Thames & Hudson, 2000.

Sullivan, Michael. *The Arts of China.* 4th ed. Berkeley: University of California Press, 1999.

Weidner, Marsha, et al. *Views from the Jade Terrace: Chinese Women Artists, 1300–1912.* New York: Rizzoli, 1988.

DAILY LIFE

Benn, Charles D. *China's Golden Age: Everyday Life in the Tang Dynasty*. New York: Oxford University Press, 2004.

Carrasco, David. *Daily Life of the Aztecs: People of the Sun and Earth*. Westport, Conn.: Greenwood, 1998.

Dunn, Charles James. *Everyday Life in Traditional Japan*. Tokyo: Tuttle, 1972.

Gies, Frances, and Joseph Gies. *Daily Life in Medieval Times: A Vivid, Detailed Account of Birth, Marriage, and Death; Food, Clothing, and Housing; Love and Labor in the Middle Ages*. New York: Black Dog and Leventhal, 1999.

Morgan, Gwyneth. *Life in a Medieval Village*. Minneapolis, Minn.: Lerner, 1982.

Picard, Lisa. *Dr. Johnson's London: Coffee-houses and Climbing Boys, Medicine, Toothpaste and Gin, Poverty and Press-gangs, Freakshows and Female Education*. New York: St. Martin's, 2001.

Rice, Earle. *Life during the Middle Ages*. San Diego, Calif.: Lucent, 1998.

FAMILY

Chatterjee, Indrani, ed. *Unfamiliar Relations: Family and History in South Asia*. New Brunswick, N.J.: Rutgers University Press, 2004.

Gies, Frances. *Marriage and the Family in the Middle Ages*. New York: Harper and Row, 1987.

Ihara Saikaku. *The Japanese Family Storehouse*. 1688. Translated by G. W. Sargent. Cambridge, England: Cambridge University Press, 1959.

Orme, Nicholas. *Medieval Children*. New Haven, Conn.: Yale University Press, 2001.

MYTHS, LEGENDS, STORIES, AND POEMS

Bertol, Roland. *Sundiata: The Epic of the Lion King*. New York: Thomas Y. Crowell, 1970.

Eisner, Will. *Sundiata: A Legend of Africa*. New York: NBM, 2002.

FitzGerald, Edward, trans. *The Rubaiyat of Omar Khayyam*. Philadelphia: Running Press, 1989.

Hodges, Margaret. *Of Swords and Sorcerers: The Adventures of King Arthur and His Knights*. New York: Scribners, 1993.

Jiang,Wei, and Cheng an Jiang. *Legend of Mu Lan: A Heroine of Ancient China*. Monterey, Calif.: Victory, 1992.

Kimmel, Eric. *Don Quixote and the Windmills*. New York: Farrar, Straus & Giroux, 2004.

Krishnaswami, Uma. *Shower of Gold: Girls and Women in the Stories of India*. North Haven, Conn.: Linnet, 1999.

Murasaki Shikibu. *The Tale of Genji*. Translated by Royall Tyler. New York: Viking, 2001.

Pyle, Howard. *King Arthur and His Knights*. 1903. Reprint, New York: Dover, 1965.

Young, Ed. *Monkey King*. New York: HarperCollins, 2001.

RELIGION AND PHILOSOPHY

Bainton, Roland, ed. *The Medieval Church*. New York: Van Nostrand, 1962.

Brown, Stephen F. *Protestantism*. New York: Facts on File, 2002.

Hindley, Geoffrey. *The Medieval Establishment, 1200–1500*. New York: Putnam, 1970.

Hinds, Kathryn. *Life in the Middle Ages: The Church*. New York: Benchmark, 2001.

Hoobler, Thomas. *Confucianism*. New York: Facts on File, 1993.

Knipe, David M. *Hinduism: Experiments in the Sacred*. San Francisco: HarperSanFrancisco, 1991.

MacCulloch, Diarmaid. *The Reformation*. New York: Viking, 2004.

McManners, John. *The Oxford Illustrated History of Christianity*. New York: Oxford University Press, 1990.

Scruton, Roger. *Kant: A Very Short Introduction*. New York: Oxford University Press, 2001.

Snelling, John. *Buddhism*. New York: Bookwright, 1986.

⟨⟨ Tappert, Theodore G., ed. *Selected Writings of Martin Luther*. Philadelphia: Fortress Press, 1967.

Thomson, Laurence G. *Chinese Religion: An Introduction*. Belmont, Calif.: Wadsworth, 1996.

Xinzhong Yao. *An Introduction to Confucianism*. Cambridge, England: Cambridge University Press, 2000.

SCIENCE AND TECHNOLOGY

Beshore, George. *Science in Early Islamic Culture*. New York: Franklin Watts, 1998.

Elman, Benjamin A. *On Their Own Terms: Science in China 1550–1900*. Cambridge, Mass.: Harvard University Press, 2005.

Henderson, Harry. *The Scientific Revolution*. San Diego, Calif.: Lucent, 1996.

Huff, Toby E. *The Rise of Early Modern Science: Islam, China, and the West*. 2nd ed. New York: Cambridge University Press, 2003.

Needham, Joseph. *Science in Traditional China*. Cambridge, Mass.: Harvard University Press, 1981.

TRADE AND EXPLORATION

Fritz. Jean. *Around the World in a Hundred Years: From Henry the Navigator to Magellan*. New York: Putnam's, 1994.

Levathes, Louise. *When China Ruled the Seas: The Treasure Fleet of the Dragon Throne. 1405–1433*. New York: Simon and Schuster, 1994.

⟨⟨ Lopez, Robert S., and Irving W. Raymond, eds. *Medieval Trade in the Mediterranean World*. New York: Columbia University Press, 1955.

Stefoff, Rebecca. *The Accidental Explorers*. New York: Oxford University Press, 1992.

Whitfield, Susan. *Life along the Silk Road*. Berkeley: University of California Press, 1999.

Wood, Frances. *The Silk Road: Two Thousand Years in the Heart of Asia*. Berkeley: University of California Press, 2002.

WAR

Bradbury, Jim. *The Routledge Companion to Medieval Warfare*. New York: Routledge, 2004.

Brewer, Paul. *Warfare in the Renaissance World*. Austin, Tex.: Raintree Steck-Vaughn, 1999.

Child, John. *The Crusades*. Chicago: Peter Bedrick, 1996.

Coolidge, Olivia. *Tales of the Crusades*. Boston: Houghton Mifflin, 1970.

Hall, Eleanor J. *Life among the Samurai*. San Diego, Calif.: Lucent, 1999.

Thomas, Hugh. *Conquest: Cortes, Montezuma, and the Fall of Old Mexico*. New York: Simon and Schuster, 1995.

WOMEN

Cosman, Madeleine Pelner. *Women at Work in Medieval Europe*. New York: Facts on File, 2000.

Hansen, Joyce. *African Princess: Amazing Lives of Africa's Royal Women*. New York: Hyperion, 2004.

Ko, Dorothy. *Every Step a Lotus: Shoes for Bound Feet*. Berkeley: University of California Press, 2001.

LaBarge, Margaret Wade. *A Small Sound of the Trumpet: Women in Medieval Times*. Boston: Beacon, 1986.

Macdonald, Fiona. *Women in Medieval Times*. Chicago: Peter Bedrick, 2000.

Meltzer, Milton. *Ten Queens: Portraits of Women of Power*. New York: Dutton, 1998.

Misra, Rekha. *Women in Mughal India, 1526–1748 A.D.* Delhi: Munshiram Manoharlal, 1967.

Robertson, Claire C., and Martin A. Klein, eds. *Women and Slavery in Africa*. Madison: University of Wisconsin Press, 1983.

Smith, Bonnie G. *Women's History in Global Perspective*. 3 vols. Urbana: University of Illinois Press, 2004–5.

WEBSITES

Early Modern Resources
www.earlymodernweb.org.uk/
This site, maintained by Sharon Howard, a British graduate student, offers links to a variety of sites about the early modern world, which she defines as roughly 1500 to 1800.

Edsitement
http://edsitement.neh.gov/
The educational site of the National Endowment for the Humanities presents world history in the form of lesson plans, which are available in both teacher and student versions. Users can select groups of lesson plans—for example, "World History—Africa" for grades 6 through 8—using pull-down menus. From here, users can access a lesson plan of interest, such as "Trekking to Timbuktu." The student lesson plans are lively and accessible and include resources such as maps, links to relevant sites, and pictures.

The Internet Sourcebooks
Sponsored by Fordham University, these sites, grouped by historical period as well as region, offer access to a wide variety of primary sources. The regional sourcebooks are included below in the categories for the specific area.

www.fordham.edu/halsall/sbook.html#index
The Medieval History Sourcebook provides primary sources on a wide variety of topics from the Catholic Church, Islam, and Jewish life to Byzantium, the Celtic world, and Italy, to name just a few. Within these categories are many subcategories that make it easy to find sources of interest.

www.fordham.edu/halsall/mod/modsbook1.html
The early modern West section of the Modern History Sourcebook offers primary sources on such topics as the Reformation, the Scientific Revolution and the Enlightenment, and the American and French Revolutions.

The Labyrinth
http://labyrinth.georgetown.edu/
Sponsored by Georgetown University, the Labyrinth is aimed toward graduate students and professional historians, but it does provide links to numerous other sites of interest. Users can browse categories such as magic and alchemy, Arthurian legends, and the Crusades, to name just a few, and from here find lots of useful information.

NetSerf
www.netserf.org/
An index to Internet resources for medieval history, NetSerf is sponsored by Catholic University. The site is broken down into useful categories such as art, music, literature, religion, and Arthurian legends. Within each category browsers will find links to sites of interest.

The Orb
http://the-orb.net/
The Orb, or the Online Reference Book for medieval studies, sponsored by the College of Staten Island, City University of New York, is mostly for college students and professional historians. The site includes original articles on medieval history, primary sources, and links to other sites, such as museums. The Orb also has a section called Medieval Studies for the Non-specialist, which has interesting and accessible articles.

PBS Teacher Source

www.pbs.org/teachersource/
The Public Broadcasting Service site offers lesson plans and activities for teachers, with nine specifically geared to the medieval and early modern world, including Islam: Empire of Faith, Vikings in America, and the Road to Timbuktu.

University of Washington Library

www.lib.washington.edu/subject/History/
tm/medieval.html
The UW library site offers links to general sites on medieval history, as well as other libraries and institutions that have made medieval manuscripts, including digital reproductions of the intricate illuminations, and works of literature available online.

AFRICA

African Voices

www.mnh.si.edu/africanvoices/
African Voices, part of the Smithsonian National Museum of Natural History's site, offers a timeline of African history from early humans to the present.

Internet African History Sourcebook

www.fordham.edu/halsall/africa/africasbook.html
Part of Fordham University's Internet Sourcebook, this site provides primary sources from African history from ancient times to the present. Subjects of interest include Africa and Islam, the slave trade, and exploration and colonization.

ART AND ARCHITECTURE

Castles of Britain

www.castles-of-britain.com/castle31.htm
The site of this organization dedicated to preserving British castles has plenty of pictures and information about castles.

Dumbarton Oaks

www.doaks.org/Byzantine.html
The website of this leading center for the study of the Byzantine Empire includes highlights from the institution's collection. The images are not accompanied by explanations, but they give one a sense of Byzantine art and culture. The site also offers links to other sources of information on the Byzantine Empire.

Metropolitan Museum of Art

www.metmuseum.org
The site of the Metropolitan Museum of Art in New York includes highlights from the museum's collections. Of particular interest are Arms and Armor, a collection of armor and weapons from around the world, and the Cloisters, dedicated to the art and architecture of medieval Europe.

ASIA

Ask Asia

www.askasia.org/
Sponsored by the Asia Society, this site designed for students and teachers includes timelines of Asian history during the early modern period and historical maps.

Internet East Asian History Sourcebook

www.fordham.edu/halsall/eastasia/
eastasiasbook.html
Part of Fordham University's Internet Sourcebook, this site provides primary sources from East Asian history from ancient times to the present. Subjects of interest include religious traditions, divided into subcategories including Buddhism, Confucianism, and Daoism; imperial China; traditional Japan; and Korea.

Internet Indian History Sourcebook

www.fordham.edu/halsall/india/indiasbook.html
Part of Fordham University's Internet Sourcebook, this site provides primary sources from Indian history from ancient times to the present. Subjects of interest include medieval India and Muslim-era India.

EUROPE

The Camelot Project
www.lib.rochester.edu/camelot/cphome.stm
Sponsored by the University of Rochester, this
site presents texts that tell the tale of King
Arthur in addition to offering basic information about the legendary ruler of England.

Decameron Web
*www.brown.edu/Departments/Italian_Studies/
dweb/dweb.shtml*
This site sponsored by the Italian studies
department at Brown University provides useful information about Italian history and the
plague and maps, in addition to information
about Boccaccio and his *Decameron*.

End of Europe's Middle Ages
*www.ucalgary.ca/applied_history/tutor/
endmiddle/*
The University of Calgary, Canada, created
this site to give students a brief overview of
the conditions at the end of Europe's Middle
Ages. The site is structured in chapters that
summarize the economic, political, religious,
and intellectual environment of the 14th and
15th centuries.

EXPLORATION

Conquistadors
www.pbs.org/conquistadors/
This section of the Public Broadcasting Service
educational site provides information on the
conquistadors Hernando Cortes, Francisco
Pizarro, and others, as well as the native peoples they conquered.

RELIGION

The Catholic Encyclopedia
www.newadvent.org/cathen/
The Catholic organization New Advent has
put the complete text of the Catholic
Encyclopedia online. Users can search on
almost any topic related to the history of the
Catholic Church and find a concise, accessible
article on the subject.

The Internet Islamic History Sourcebook
www.fordham.edu/halsall/islam/islamsbook.html
Part of Fordham University's Internet
Sourcebook, this site provides primary sources
from Islamic history from the origins of the
faith to present times. Subjects of interest
include Islamic empire and expansion, the
caliphates, and historical maps of Islam.

The Internet Jewish History Sourcebook
www.fordham.edu/halsall/jewish/jewishsbook.html
Part of Fordham University's Internet
Sourcebook, this site provides primary sources
from Jewish history from ancient times to the
present. The section called the Jewish Middle
Ages is broken down into many useful subcategories to aid students in locating subjects of
interest.

WOMEN

The Internet Women's History Sourcebook
*www.fordham.edu/halsall/women/
womensbook.html*
Part of Fordham University's Internet
Sourcebook, this site provides primary sources
on women's history from ancient times to the
modern era. The medieval section has sources
for great women such as Joan of Arc and
Queen Eleanor, women writers, women saints,
courtly love, and daily life, among others.

THEMATIC INDEX

SERIES INDEX

Page references are grouped by volume. The abbreviations used for each volume are **AME** (*The African and Middle Eastern World*), **AS** (*The Asian World*), **EMP** (*An Age of Empires*), **EU** (*The European World*), **PS** (*Primary Sources and Reference Volume*), **SCI** (*An Age of Science and Revolutions*), **VOY** (*An Age of Voyages*). These abbreviations are also provided in the key at the bottom of the page spread.

References to illustrations and their captions are indicated by page numbers in **bold**

TEXT CREDITS

TEXT CREDITS

1. St. Jerome, *Epistolae* 123, 15; English translation in *The Medieval Church,* ed. Roland Bainton (Princeton, N.J.: Van Nostrand, 1962), 89–90.

2. Gelasius I, *Edict X,* 494, in *The Medieval Church,* ed. Bainton, 108.

3. Oddr Snorrason, *King Oláf's Saga,* in *The Viking Achievement: The Society and Culture of Early Medieval Scandinavia,* eds. Peter Foote and David M. Wilson, (London: Sidgwick and Jackson, 1978), 250–51.

4. "Lullabye," in *Religious Lyrics of the XIVth Century,* ed. Carleton Brown (Oxford: Oxford University Press, 1924); reprinted in *The Medieval Church,* ed. Bainton, 147.

5. Raymond of Agiles, "The Deeds of the Franks (1100–1101)," in *Parallel Source Problems in Medieval History,* ed. August. C. Krey (New York: Harper, 1912); reprinted in *The Medieval Church,* ed. Bainton, 118–19.

6. John of Salisbury, *Policraticus,* trans. J. Dickinson (New York: Knopf, 1927); reprinted in *The Medieval Reader,* eds. James Bruce Ross and Mary Martin McLaughlin (New York: Viking, 1949), 47–48.

7. V. Mortet, ed., *Recueil de textes relatifs à l'histoire de l'architecture en France, XIe et XIIe siècles* (Paris: A. Picard, 1911); English translation in *The Medieval Reader,* eds. Ross and McLaughlin, 539.

8. "Student Life in the College of the Sorbonne," in *University Records and Life in the Middle Ages,* ed. Lynn Thorndike (New York: Columbia University Press, 1944) 88–89.

9. Edward II, "Parliamentary Summons in England, 1295," in *Selections from Sources of English History, Being a Supplement to Text-books of English History B.C. 55–A.D. 1832,* ed. Charles W. Colby (New York: Longmans, 1905), 88–90.

10. Eileen Power, ed. and trans., *The Goodman of Paris: A Treatise on Moral and Domestic Economy by a Citizen of Paris* (London: George Routledge, 1928), 171, 173–74.

11. Al-Mas'udi, Muruj al-Dhahab wa Ma'adin al-Jawhar; French translation, *Les prairies d'or,* by Charles-Adrien-Casimir Barbier de Meynard and Abel Pavet de Courteille, ed. Charles Pellat (Paris: Société asiatique, 1962–1971); English translation in *The East African Coast: Select Documents from the First to the Earlier Nineteenth Century,* 2nd ed., ed. and trans. G. S. P. Freeman-Grenville (London: Rex Collings, 1975), 15–16.

12. Arthur J. Arberry, trans., *Poems of al-Mutanabbi* (London: Cambridge University Press, 1967); reprinted in *The Islamic World,* ed. William McNeill and Marilyn Waldman (New York: Oxford University Press, 1973), 172–73.

13. 'Ubayd 'Abd Allah b. 'Abd al-'Aziz al-Bakri, *Kitab al-masalik wa-'l-mamalik,* ed. and trans. Baron MacGuckin de Slane as *Déscription de l'Afrique Septentrionale* (Algiers: A. Jourdan, 1911); English translation in *Corpus of Early Arabic Sources for West African History,* trans. J. F. P. Hopkins and ed. N. Levtzion and J. F. P. Hopkins (Cambridge, England: Cambridge University Press, 1981), 79–80.

14. Usama ibn Munqidh, "Memoirs," in *The Islamic World,* ed. McNeill and Waldman, 203–4.

15. Abu 'Abd Allah Muhammad al-sharif al-Idrisi, *The Pleasure of Him Who Longs To Cross the Horizons*; English translation in *Corpus of Early Arabic Sources for West African History,* trans. Hopkins and ed. Levtzion and Hopkins, 118.

16. Omar Khayyám, *Rubáiyát,* trans. Edward FitzGerald (New York: St. Martin's, 1983); reprinted in *Worlds of History: A Comparative Reader, Volume One: To 1550,* ed. Kevin Reilly (Boston: Bedford/St. Martin's, 1974), 300–1.

17. Benjamin of Tudela, "The Travels of Rabbi Benjamin of Tudela," in *Early Travels in Palestine,* ed. Thomas Wright (London: Bohn, 1848), 74–76.

18. Maurice Delafosse, ed., *Notes Africaines* (Dakar: Institut Français d'Afrique Noire, 1959); English translation in *African Civilization Revisited: From Antiquity to Modern Times,* ed. Basil Davidson (Trenton, N.J.: Africa World Press, 1991), 90–91.

19. Muhammad Mujir Wajib Adib, *The Key to Paradise,* in *Sources of Indian Tradition,* vol. 1, ed. William Theodore de Bary et al. (New York: Columbia University Press, 1958), 386–87.

20. Djeli Mamadou Kouyate as recorded by Djibril Tamsir Niane, ed., *Sundiata: An Epic of Old Mali,* trans. G. D. Pickett (London: Longmans, 1965); reprinted in *African Civilization Revisited: From Antiquity to Modern Times,* ed. Davidson, 88–89.

21. Mahmud Kati, *Tarikh al-Fettash,* ed. Octave Houdas (Paris: E. Leroux, 1913); English translation in *African Civilization Revisited: From Antiquity to Modern Times,* ed. Davidson, 114–15.

22. *Lankavatara Sutra,* English translation in *Sources of Indian Tradition,* ed. William Theodore de Bary et al. (New York: Columbia University Press, 1958), 1:169–70.

23. Hwui Li, *The Life of Hiuen-Tsiang,* trans. S. Beal (London, 1911; 2nd ed., Delhi: Munshiram Manoharlal, 1973); reprinted in Sally Hovey Wriggins, *Xuanzang: A Buddhist Pilgrim on the Silk Road* (Boulder, Co.: Westview, 1996), 15, 75.

24. Du Fu, "At the Corner of the World," in *Poems of the Late T'ang,* trans. A. C. Graham (London: Penguin, 1965), 44.

25. Patricia Buckley Ebrey, ed. and trans., "The *Book of Filial Piety for Women* Attributed to a Woman Née Zheng (ca. 730)," in *Under Confucian Eyes: Writings on Gender in Chinese History,* eds. Susan Mann and Yu-Yin Cheng (Berkeley: University of California Press, 2001), 50–54.

26. Murasaki Shikibu, *The Tale of Genji,* trans. Arthur Waley (Tokyo: Charles E. Tuttle, 1972), 1:500–1.

27. Ratanbai, "Song," in *Women Writing in India 600 B.C. to the Present,* eds. Susie Tharu and K. Lalita (New York: HarperCollins, 1993), 1:386–87.

28. Francesco di Balduccio Pegolotti, *Guide for Merchants,* English translation in *Medieval Trade in the Mediterranean World,* eds. Robert S. Lopez and Irving W. Raymond (New York: Columbia University Press, 1955), 355–57.

29. Gao Qi, "Caicha ci," in *Daquan ji* (reprint, Taipei: Shangwu yinshuguan, 1986); English translation in Weijing Lu, "Poems on Tea-Picking," in *Under Confucian Eyes: Writings on Gender in Chinese History,* eds. Mann and Cheng, 233–35.

30. King Munjong, "Edict on Irrigation Works," in *Sources of Korean Tradition: From Early Times through the Sixteenth Century,* eds. Peter H. Lee and William Theodore de Bary (New York: Columbia University Press, 1997), 1:333.

31. *Anonymous Gujarati, "My Courtyard Has Been Cleaned and Plastered,"* trans. *Nita Ramaiya,* in Women Writing in India, 600 B.C. to the Present, *eds.*

Susie Tharu and K. Lalita (London: Pandora, 1991), 139–40.

32. 'Ala' al-Din 'Ata-Malik Juvaini, *The History of the World Conqueror,* translated by John Andrew Boyle (Manchester, England: Manchester University Press, 1958); reprinted in *The Islamic World,* ed. William H. McNeill and Marilyn Robinson Waldman (New York: Oxford University Press, 1973), 263–65.

33. Anonymous, *Crónica incompleta de los Reyes Catolicos (1469–1476), segun un manuscrito anónino de la época,* ed. Julio Puyol (Madrid,1934); trans. Warren H. Carroll, *Isabel of Spain: The Catholic Queen* (Front Royal, Va.: Christendom Press, 1991), 35.

34. Christopher Columbus, "Columbus's Impression of the New World," in *Readings in European History,* ed. and trans. Leon Bernard and Theodore B. Hodges (New York: Macmillan, 1958), 218–19.

35. Hans Mayr, "The Sack of Kilwa and Mombasa: An Eye-Witness Account of 1505," in *Corpus of Early Arabic Sources for West Africa History,* trans. J. F. P. Hopkins and ed. N. Levtzion and J. F. P. Hopkins (Cambridge, England: Cambridge University Press, 1981), 109.

36. Anonymous, "Povyest o Gyurgyu Zrnoyevichu, narechenom Skenderbegu," manuscript no. 418, in Chedomil Mijatovich, *Constantine: The Last Emperor of the Greeks or the Conquest of Constantinople by the Turks* (London: Sampson Low, Marston, 1892), 41–43.

37. Anonymous, *Annals of Tlatelolco,* part 5; trans. Gordon Brotherston, *Image of the New World: The American Continent Portrayed in Native Texts* (London: Thames and Hudson, 1979), 34–35.

38. "Memorandum on the Korean Expedition", in Nisshi kosho-shi kenkyu, 55–57; trans. in *Sources of the Japanese Tradition,* ed. Ryusaku Tsunoda et al. (New York: Columbia University Press, 1958), 327–28.

39. Bada'uni, *Muntakhah ut-Tawarikh* (History of Islam); trans. in *Sources of Indian Tradition,* ed. William Theodore de Bary (New York: Columbia University Press, 1958), 1:432–34.

40. Alexander Radishchev, "A Journey from St. Petersburg to Moscow," in *Connecting with the Past, Volume II: From 1320* (Lexington, Mass.: D. C. Heath, 1995), 2:504.

41. Anonymous, "The Reformation of the Emperor Sigismund (Basel, c.1438)," in *Documents on the Continental Reformation,* ed. and trans. William G. Naphy (New York: St. Martin's, 1996), 7–8.

42. Muhammad ibn Asad Jalal ud-din al-Dawwani, *Jalali's Ethics,* in William Theodore de Bary et al., *Sources of Indian Tradition,* (New York: Columbia University Press, 1958), 1:503–4.

43. Thomas Malory, *Le Morte Darthur or The Hoole Book of Kyng Arthur and of His Noble Knyghtes of the Rounde Table,* 1485. Reprint (London: Dent, 1967), 71.

44. Desiderius Erasmus, *Opus Epistolarum Des. Erasmi Roterodami,* ed. H. M. Allen et al. (Oxford: Clarendon, 1906–58), EE 288. Trans. Marcus A. Haworth, *Erasmus and His Age: Selected Letters of Desiderius Erasmus,* ed. Hans J. Hillerbrand (New York: Harper and Row, 1970), 66–67.

45. Albrecht Dürer, "Tagebuch der Reise in die Niederlande" [1520], trans. in *The Portable Renaissance Reader,* ed. James Bruce Ross and Mary Martin McLaughlin (New York: Penguin, 1978), 228–30.

46. Martin Luther, *Luther's Works: Volume 54, Table Talk,* ed. and trans. Theodore G. Tappert (Philadelphia: Fortress, 1967), 160–61, 174–75, 222–23, 317.

47. John Calvin, "Conversion and Call to Geneva," trans. in *Introduction to Contemporary Civilization in the West,* ed. contemporary civilization staff of Columbia College (New York: Columbia University Press, 1960), 110–11.

48. Launoy, "Fernando of Cordova, the Boy Wonder," in *University Records and Life in the Middle Ages,* trans. Lynn Thorndike (New York: Columbia University Press, 1949), 341–42.

49. Niccolò Machiavelli, *The Prince,* trans. in *Readings in European History,* ed. Leon Bernard and Theodore B. Hodges (New York: Macmillan, 1958), 208–9.

50. Wu Ch'eng-en, *Monkey,* trans. Arthur Waley, 1942. Reprint (London: Unwin, 1984), 177, 178–79.

51. Miguel de Cervantes, *The Ingenious Hidalgo Don Quixote de la Mancha,* trans. John Rutherford (New York: Penguin, 2001), 63–64.

52. Yang Szu-ch'ang, "The Dragon Boat Race," in *Chinese Civilization and Society: A Sourcebook,* ed. Patricia Buckley Ebrey (New York: Free Press, 1981), 133–35.

53. Samuel Pepys, *Diary of Samuel Pepys* (London: Simpkin, Marshall, Hamilton, Kent, 1825), "Samuel Pepys Describes the Great London Fire, 1666," reprinted in *Readings in European History,* ed. Leon Bernard and Theodore B. Hodges (New York: Macmillan,1958), 292–93.

54. Count Lorenzo Magalotti, *Travels of Cosmo, Grand Duke of Tuscany* (London: J. Mawman, 1821), 185–89, reprinted in *English Historical Documents, 1660–1714,* 2nd ed., ed. Andrew Browning (London: Routledge, 1979), 481–82.

55. Louis XIV, Revocation of the Edict of Nantes, 1685, trans. in James Harvey Robinson, *Readings in European History* (Boston: Ginn, 1904–6), 289–91.

56. Sor Juana Inés de la Cruz, *Respuesta a Sor Filotea* (Reply to Sister Philothea), 1691, in *Fama y obras póstumas* (Madrid, 1700), reprinted in *Obras selectas,* ed. Georgina Savat de Rivers and Elias L. Rivers (Barcelona: Noguer, 1976), trans. in *A Sor Juana Anthology,* ed. Alan S. Trueblood (Cambridge, Mass.: Harvard University Press, 1988), 208–10, reprinted in *Women's Political and Social Thought: An Anthology,* ed. Hilda L. Smith and Berenice A. Carroll (Bloomington: Indiana University Press, 2000), 92–94.

57. Antoine Galland, *De l'origine and du progrès du café,* 1699. Reprint (Paris: Editions La Bibliothèque, 1992), 59–61, trans. Bonnie G. Smith.

58. Phillis Wheatley, "On Being Brought from Africa to America," *Poems on Various Subjects, Religious and Moral* (London: Archibald Bell, 1773); reprinted in *Women's Political and Social Thought: An Anthology,* ed. Hilda L. Smith and Berenice Carroll (Bloomington: Indiana University Press, 2000), 125.

59. Immanuel Kant, "Beantwortung der Frage: Was Ist Aufklärung," in *Berlinische Monatsschrift* 4 (1784), 481–94; trans. Mary C. Smith, "What Is Enlightenment?" in *Introduction to Contemporary Civilization in the West,* 3rd ed. (New York: Columbia University Press, 1960), 1,071–72.

60. Sugita Gempaku, "A Dutch Anatomy Lesson in Japan," 1771, in Kevin Reilly, ed., *Worlds of History: A Comparative Reader,* vol. 2 (Boston: Bedford/St. Martin's, 2000), 152–53.

61. Declaration of the Rights of Man and of the Citizen, trans. in *Readings in European History,* ed. Robinson, 409–11.

62. Toussaint L'Ouverture, "Letter to the Haitian Blacks," English translation in *The Black Jacobins,* ed. C. L. R. James (New York: Vintage, 1963), 125.

DONALD R. KELLEY is the James Westfall Thompson Professor of History at Rutgers University. He is the author of many books and articles about legal, religious, intellectual, and cultural history, including *Historians and the Law in Revolutionary France, Versions of History from Antiquity to the Enlightenment,* and his most recent work, *The Descent of Ideas.* He is the executive editor of the *Journal of the History of Ideas* and an elected member of the American Philosophical Society and the American Academy of Arts and Sciences.

BONNIE G. SMITH is Board of Governors Professor of History at Rutgers University. She has edited a series for teachers on Women's and Gender History in Global Perspective for the American Historical Association and has served as chair of the test development committee for the Advanced Placement examination in European history. Professor Smith is the author of many books on European, comparative, and women's history, among them *Confessions of a Concierge* and *Imperialism: A History in Documents.* She is co-author of *The Making of the West: Peoples and Cultures,* editor in chief of the forthcoming Oxford encyclopedia on women in world history, and general editor of an Oxford world history series for high school students and general readers.